150 NIFTY

CRAFTS, MAGIC TRICKS & SCIENCE EXPERIMENTS

Written by
Cambria Cohen, Elizabeth Wood,
Lisa Melton, and Eric Ladizinsky

Illustrated by Neal Yamamoto

BARNES
& NOBLE
BOOKS
NEW YORK

CONTENTS

Magical Sand Art

The main ingredient in this fun craft is something the world will never run out of: sand! If you don't live near a beach, collect sand from your nearby playground or park.

What You'll Need

- 9 empty glass jars or glass bottles (with lids or caps)
- powder paints, various colors
- a funnel (optional)
- sand, enough to fill the jars

Directions

1. Start by filling eight of the jars half full with sand.
2. Pick a color of powder paint and pour some of it into one of the jars. Cover the jar tightly and shake it well. The paint will color the sand.
3. Repeat step 2 with a different color paint and a different jar of sand. Do the same with the remaining jars, putting one color of paint in each.
4. Now take the empty jar. Pick one color of sand and pour it into the empty jar to create a 1" layer. (Use the funnel if you are pouring into a bottle.)
5. Choose a different color and pour another layer on top of the previous one, creating a ½" layer. Continue with the remaining colors of sand, varying the thickness of each layer. When the jar is full, put the lid on tightly. You've got a beautiful sand "sculpture."

NOTE: The paint tube and number in the upper right-hand corner indicate the level of difficulty of each craft, 1 being the easiest, 3 being the hardest.

Walking on Eggshells

Did you know you can dress up bottles, boxes, and cans with crushed egg-shells? It's eggs-traordinary!

What You'll Need

- a dozen raw eggs
- a large mixing bowl
- a glass bottle, shoebox, or tin can
- a needle
- newspaper
- tempera paints, various colors
- glue
- a paintbrush

Directions

1. Blow out the insides of the eggs first. Hold an egg over the mixing bowl. Make a hole in one end of the egg with the needle. Then make a hole in the other end, but don't take the needle out. Move the needle around inside the egg till the hole is about ½″ wide. Remove the needle. Blow through the smaller hole. The inside of the egg will come out of the bigger hole. Rinse out the egg with cool water and repeat with the remaining eggs. (Don't throw the insides away—cook them for breakfast!)
2. Spread out a few sheets of newspaper and put the empty shells on top. Cover them with another sheet of newspaper. Now get your shoes on and stomp all over the shells to crush them. When you're through, take off the top sheet of newspaper.
3. Put glue all over the bottle, shoebox, or can. Then roll it in the crushed eggshells, making sure it gets completely covered. Let the glue dry.
4. Finally, use the tempera paints to paint the eggshells. Make stripes, polka dots, zig-zag patterns . . . use your imagination!

3

Home Sweet Home

Let your imagination go wild as you build your own custom-made home!

What You'll Need

- 2 boxes of sugar cubes
- construction paper, various colors
- a 12″ x 12″ piece of cardboard
- a 10″ x 10″ piece of cardboard
- cellophane (or plastic wrap)
- colored paper napkins
- newspaper
- glue or rubber cement
- a ruler
- scissors
- thread
- tape
- sandpaper
- a pencil

Directions

1. First, lay down some newspaper and put the larger piece of cardboard on it. Form a rectangle out of sugar cubes in the middle of the cardboard. The rectangle should be 10 cubes long and about 6 cubes wide. Glue the cubes together. Now glue on a second row, then a third, building upward.
2. To make windows, just omit one or two cubes from two consecutive rows to make an open square. Leave an open rectangle for the front door.
3. Stop when the house is six rows high. Now add the finishing touches! To cover the windows, cut out a square of cellophane and tape it over the windows from the *inside* of the house. Cut curtains out of paper napkins. Glue them to the inside of the windows and tie them back with thread.
4. Cut a roof out of the smaller pieces of cardboard and fold it in half to make an upside-down "V." Set the roof over the house and glue it in place.
5. Finally, cut a straight or curved walkway out of sandpaper and glue it down so that it leads to the front door, which you can make out of construction paper. "Landscape" your house by cutting green construction paper for the lawn, trees, and bushes!

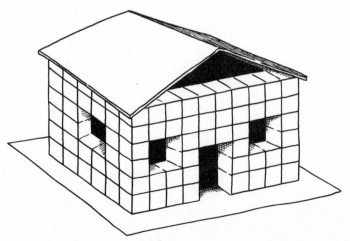

Sublime Chimes

Making beautiful music is a "breeze" with these cool wind chimes!

What You'll Need

- 2 pieces of heavy cardboard, at least 16" x 6" large
- several sheets of light cardboard
- 3 or 4 fifty-cent coins
- scissors
- string
- old silverware
- tape
- a ruler
- 2 or 3 metal lids
- large nails
- old keys
- a pencil

Directions

1. Start by making a holder for your chimes. Cut two triangles out of the heavy cardboard. The base of the triangles should be 16", and the height about 6".
2. Find the midpoint at the bottom of the first triangle and cut a 3" vertical slot. Then, from the top point of the second triangle, cut a 3" vertical slot.
3. Now use the scissors to punch a row of holes, about 1" apart, across the bottom of each triangle. The holes should be ¼" from the bottom edge.
4. Next, take the first triangle and slide it into the slot on the second triangle (A). Glue them in place if necessary.
5. Cut several 4" x 1" strips of light cardboard, one for each hole you punched in the heavy cardboard. Use the scissors to poke a hole at the end of each strip.

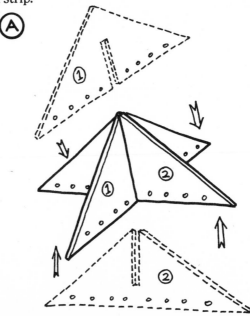

6. Now cut several 12″ pieces of string. Tape the end of each string to a lid, coin, or piece of silverware. For the keys, thread the string through the hole and tie a knot. For the nails, wind the string around the nail under the head so it will hold.

7. Attach each chime to a strip of cardboard. Thread the free end of each piece of string through one hole and out the opposite hole in each strip (B).

8. Next, take the free end of each string again, put it through a hole in the heavy cardboard holder, and tie a big knot to secure it.

9. Poke a hole at the top of the cardboard holder. Thread a 12″ piece of string through the hole and tie the ends together for hanging (B).

One Step Further

Next time you're at the beach, collect seashells to make into a pretty wind chime! Or try using small glass jars, such as baby food jars or pimiento jars, instead of metal objects.

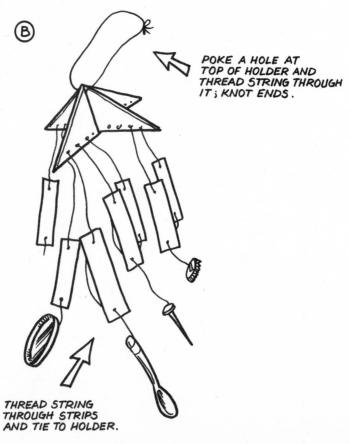

(B)

POKE A HOLE AT TOP OF HOLDER AND THREAD STRING THROUGH IT; KNOT ENDS.

THREAD STRING THROUGH STRIPS AND TIE TO HOLDER.

Works Like a Charm!

With just a few charms and simple trinkets, you can make a personal gift for your best friend or a member of your family!

What You'll Need

- small personal objects such as hair clips, buttons, perfume bottles, beads, plastic figures, erasers, rubber animals
- popsicle sticks (available at craft stores)
- frame stand (optional)
- plastic, silver, or gold charms
- glue
- newspaper

Directions

1. To make the frame, glue 16 popsicle sticks, edge to edge, into a flat square shape, four on each side. Overlap and glue the inner 4 sticks at each corner (A). Then turn the frame over and glue popsicle sticks flat, edge to edge, to create a solid back (B).
2. Now make it charming! Lay the frame on a sheet of newspaper. Glue a charm or object onto the frame. Pick another object and glue it next to the first one.
3. Continue gluing objects. Work on alternate sides of the frame so that one side can dry while you're working on another one. Cover as much of the frame as possible.
4. Let the frame dry completely. Then, insert a photograph of the person who will receive the frame! Trim the photo if necessary.

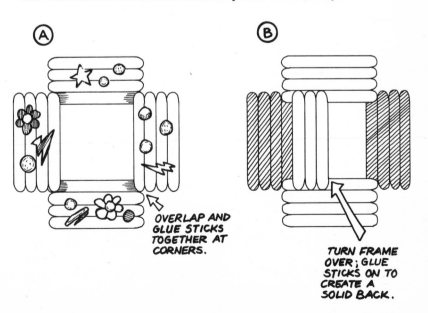

Ⓐ

OVERLAP AND GLUE STICKS TOGETHER AT CORNERS.

Ⓑ

TURN FRAME OVER; GLUE STICKS ON TO CREATE A SOLID BACK.

6 Zoetrope

Invented in the 1830s, the zoetrope (ZOH-uh-trohp) was an early motion-picture gadget. When it was rotated, a short movie strip came to life inside! Here's how to make a miniature version of your own.

What You'll Need

- colored pencils or markers
- black construction paper
- light cardboard
- a paper cup with a flat bottom
- a small bead
- scissors or hobby knife
- a compass
- a ruler
- cellophane tape
- a paper clip

Directions

1. Start by making your filmstrip. Cut a strip of cardboard 13″ long and about 1½″ wide. On one side of the strip, draw a moving-picture scene using the pencils or markers. You can draw a person doing cartwheels, a frog jumping, or a bird flying. When you're done, tape the ends together to form a ring, with the scene you drew on the inside of the ring.

2. To make the zoetrope, cut a strip of black construction paper 13½″ long and 3″ wide. Lay the strip horizontally. Place the ruler along the top edge. Starting at one end, make a mark at $^{15}/_{16}$″, then 1″, then $1^{15}/_{16}$″, then 2″, and so on. Continue doing this all the way across the top of the strip (A).

3. Now you're going to cut slits out of the narrow areas that measure $^{1}/_{16}$″. It might be best to use the hobby knife for this. The slits should not go farther than 1″ down. Use the ruler to help you cut straight.

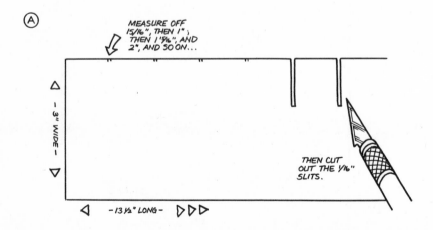

(A) MEASURE OFF 15/16", THEN 1", THEN 1 15/16", AND 2", AND SO ON...

– 3" WIDE –

THEN CUT OUT THE 1/16" SLITS.

◁ – 13 ½" LONG – ▷ ▷ ▷

4. To create flaps across the bottom of the strip, cut a row of notches across the bottom edge. The notches should be ¼" high. Each notch should match up with each slit above (B).
5. Fold up the flaps. Tape the ends of the strip together to form a ring. Make sure the flaps are on the inside of the ring.
6. To make the base of your zoetrope, use the compass to draw a circle with a 4¼" diameter on another piece of cardboard. Cut out the circle and drop it into the ring. The circle should rest on the flaps at the bottom of the ring. Turn the zoetrope over and tape the flaps onto the base (C). Flip the zoetrope right side up again.
7. Now set the paper cup on your work surface, bottom side up. Unbend the paper clip to form a "P" shape. Poke the stem of the clip through the center of the zoetrope base. Slide the bead onto the stem and push the clip through the center of the cup (D).
8. Drop your filmstrip ring into the zoetrope ring. Position yourself so that you are eye level with the zoetrope. Use your hand to spin the ring. Look through the slits between the black squares. You'll see a moving picture! Try creating a whole bunch of filmstrips and watch them come to life in your new zoetrope!

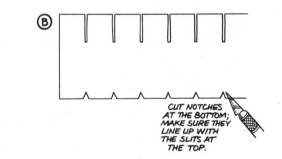

Ⓑ

CUT NOTCHES
AT THE BOTTOM;
MAKE SURE THEY
LINE UP WITH
THE SLITS AT
THE TOP.

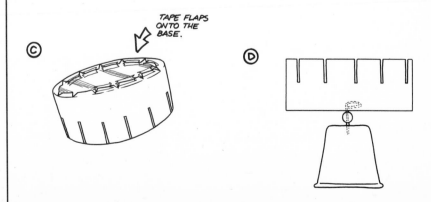

TAPE FLAPS
ONTO THE
BASE.

Ⓒ

Ⓓ

Burning the Midnight Oil

PARENTAL SUPERVISION REQUIRED
With just a few simple tools, you can make beautiful floating lamps that will impress your friends!

What You'll Need

- a wine cork
- a sharp knife
- a clear, shallow bowl, wine glass, or glass jar
- tweezers
- scissors
- entire wick from an old candle
- salad oil
- matches
- a nail
- a ruler

Directions

1. To begin, use the knife to cut your wine cork into slices about ⅛″ thick (A).
2. Carefully poke the nail through the center of each slice. Try not to crumble the cork!
3. Next, use the scissors to cut the wick into pieces ½″ long.
4. String each wick piece through the hole in each cork slice. Fray each wick at one end by pulling apart the string and flattening it against the cork (A). This will prevent the wick from coming out.
5. Keep in mind that the shape of the bowl, glass, or jar you choose will make these lamps look unique. Fill the bowl, glass, or jar half full with water.
6. Now pour enough salad oil on top of the water to make a ½″ layer.
7. Float the cork slices on the water, frayed part of the wick down, and light them (B). If the glass is too deep, hold a match in a pair of tweezers and reach down inside the glass. ASK A PARENT TO HELP YOU!

Ⓐ

CUT THE CORK INTO ⅛″ SLICES.

FRAY THE END OF THE WICK.

Ⓑ

Marvelous Marbleized Stationery

Once you've turned plain white paper into stunning stationery, you won't want to write on anything else!

What You'll Need

- white typing paper
- a disposable baking pan (larger than the paper)
- newspaper
- white envelopes
- clean rags
- pencils
- enamel oil paints (2 or 3 colors)

Directions

1. First, lay some sheets of newspaper on the table. Fill the baking pan about three-quarters full with water and place it on the newspaper.
2. Now choose an oil paint. (If you use more than three colors, your stationery will look too muddy.) Dip the pointed end of the pencil into the paint, then hold the pencil over the pan and let the paint dribble into the water (A). Repeat, using a different pencil for each color.
3. Next, "pull" the paint into different shapes by lightly running the pointed end of a clean pencil (one that doesn't have paint on it) through the water. Swirl the pencil around until you have a design you like.
4. Take a sheet of paper and carefully lay it on top of the water. Wait just a few seconds, then pick up the paper by a corner and pull it out of the water (B).

13

5. Lay the paper, paint side up, on a clean rag and let it dry overnight. Do your writing on the white side, so the marble design is on the back.
6. No stationery set is complete without matching envelopes! You can marbleize the whole front or just the back flap. Repeat steps 4 and 5 with a plain white envelope. If you want to marbleize only the flap, bend it up and, holding the envelope by the bottom, lay the flap on the water-and-paint mixture and pull it out.

One Step Further

Try mixing and matching colors. You can also make a marbleized journal or diary by inserting blank white sheets in between two painted sheets. Make sure the painted sides face out. Punch holes in the upper and lower left-hand corners, then "bind" your diary with string or yarn.

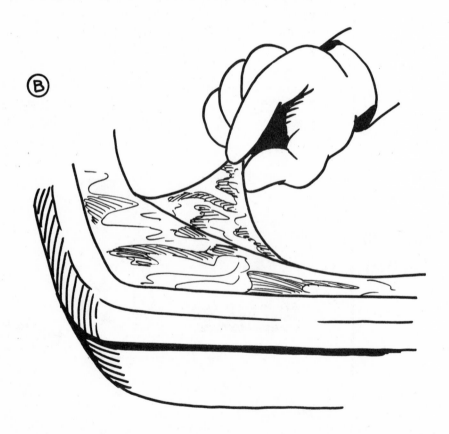

9

It's a Piñata!

Here's a craft that's as much fun to wreck as it is to make!

What You'll Need

- a large balloon
- liquid laundry starch
- tempera paint, various colors
- tissue paper, various colors

- newspaper
- a paintbrush
- assorted candies
- a screw ring
- a cup
- string

- masking tape
- glue
- scissors
- pin or needle
- water

Directions

1. Start by blowing up the balloon and tying a knot.
2. To papier-mâché the balloon, tear a few sheets of newspaper into wide strips. Mix $\frac{2}{3}$ starch and $\frac{1}{3}$ water in a cup. Place a strip of newspaper over the balloon. Dip the paintbrush into the starch mixture and "paint" over the strip (A). Cover the whole balloon, but leave a hole around the knot that's big enough to fit the candy in. Let the balloon dry.
3. Pop the balloon with a pin near the knot. Shake out the balloon pieces.
4. Fill the papier-mâché balloon with candy. Cover the opening with tape.
5. Now paint your piñata in bright colors. Try gluing strips of tissue paper on each end to make your piñata look like a giant piece of wrapped candy!
6. Carefully insert the screw ring into the middle of the piñata. Put a string through the ring and hang the piñata from a tree in your backyard or from a basketball hoop if you have one (B).

One Step Further

Try papier-mâchéing several balloons together in the shape of an animal. Add cardboard for ears, a starched string for a tail, and strips of tissue paper for hair.

Ⓐ PLACE NEWSPAPER STRIPS ON BALLOON; PAINT OVER WITH STARCH MIXTURE.

Ⓑ

Become a Master Caster!

Here's how to make a perfect plaster cast of your hand! It's not as difficult as it looks!

What You'll Need

- a 10-pound bag of plaster of Paris (available at hardware or paint stores)
- two large mixing bowls
- a wooden spoon
- a shallow baking pan

- petroleum jelly
- a measuring cup
- wax paper
- dishwashing liquid
- hammer and chisel
- water

- pliers
- glue
- a teacup
- newspaper
- a paintbrush

Directions

1. First, make a mold for your cast. Lay down several sheets of newspaper to catch any plaster drippings.
2. Fill the bowl with one pint of water. Open the bag of plaster. Use the teacup to scoop out the plaster and *slowly* sprinkle it into the bowl of water. The plaster will start to absorb the water. DON'T STIR YET! Keep adding scoops of plaster until all the water is absorbed (it should take about eight teacups full) and the mixture looks like oatmeal.
3. *Now* stir with the spoon for three minutes. The plaster will begin to thicken.
4. Rub petroleum jelly all over the hand you're going to cast (the hand you do not write with), and place the hand on a large piece of wax paper, palm side down.

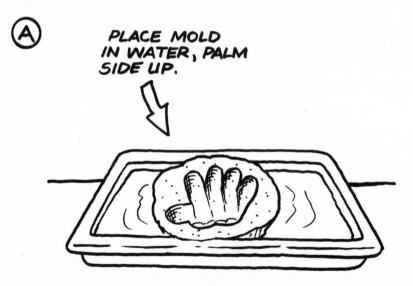

Ⓐ PLACE MOLD IN WATER, PALM SIDE UP.

5. Have a friend or parent use the teacup to scoop out the plaster mixture and pour it over your hand. Keep your hand pressed flat so no plaster gets underneath.

6. After your hand is completely covered, wait a few minutes until the plaster in the bowl thickens a bit and starts to look like sour cream. Then scoop out enough plaster to make a 1″ layer on your hand. Now wait 10 more minutes while the plaster dries. Ask your mom or dad to clean out the bowl for you before the leftover plaster dries.

7. When the plaster over your hand starts to feel warm, wiggle your fingers and slowly pull your hand out. The chunk of plaster that is left is your mold! If some of the mold breaks off when you pull out your hand, just glue the pieces back together.

8. Next, put a squirt of dishwashing liquid in another bowl and add some water to make it soapy. Then fill the shallow baking pan with water. Turn the mold over so the hand imprint is facing up. Use the paintbrush to "paint" the hand imprint with soapy water (which will make it easier to chip off the mold later). Place the mold, hand side up, in the pan of water so that only the outside of the mold gets wet (A). Hold it there for about five minutes. The outside of the mold must be *completely* saturated, or else it will absorb too much water out of the fresh batch of plaster that you will pour to make the cast.

Ⓑ

POUR PLASTER INTO MOLD; POUR UNTIL IT BUILDS TO 1″ ABOVE THE MOLD.

9. Take out the mold and lay it on a sheet of wax paper, hand side up. Mix another batch of plaster and, when the plaster starts to get stiff, carefully pour it into the mold, filling the fingertips. Keep pouring the plaster so that it builds up to about 1″ above the mold to create a base (B). Let the plaster harden; it will take at least an hour.

10. Now you need to remove the mold. You can use the pliers to break off pieces around the edge, but you'll have to use the hammer and chisel to chip away most of the mold (C). Ask an adult to help you!

11. Once the mold has been removed, soak the hand cast in some soapy water and let it dry. If you need to patch any gouges or chips, just mix a little plaster and water and fill the cracks. You've made a "hands-down" masterpiece!

One Step Further

You can shellac, varnish, or paint your plaster cast any way you want. Next time, try making a cast of your foot! Sand down the heel so that the foot stands upright with the toes pointed up. Then make another foot cast and use the two casts as bookends (or would that be foot-ends?)! Go outside and try pouring plaster into tire tracks or animal footprints you find in the mud or dirt. When the plaster hardens, lift it up. You should get an impression of the track!

©

CAREFULLY CHIP AWAY MOLD.

Playing It Safe

You can turn an ordinary book into a special safe that only you know about!

What You'll Need

- an old hardcover book
- rubber cement
- a hobby knife
- a pencil
- a ruler

Directions

1. First, find an old hardcover book, about 200 pages long, that no one wants. Open up the book to the first page.
2. Take the pencil and ruler and mark 1″ from all four sides of the page. Then connect the marks by drawing a rectangle.
3. Now use the ruler and the hobby knife to cut out the shape you just drew, leaving the 1″ border.
4. Repeat steps 2 and 3 with the remaining pages until the middle sections have all been cut out. Be patient—this may take awhile. Try cutting at least 3 or 4 pages at a time. When you're done, you should have a rectangle-shaped empty space inside the book!
5. Brush rubber cement along the four walls that line the empty space. This will hold the pages together. Let the rubber cement dry.
6. Now you have a place to hide your valuables! You can put money, secret messages, keys, or jewelry in the special compartment. When you close the book and put it on your bookshelf, no one will know it's a safe—except you!

BRUSH CEMENT ON INSIDE FOUR WALLS TO HOLD THE PAGES TOGETHER.

Up Periscope!

With this periscope, you'll be able to look over things and around corners!

What You'll Need

- a tall, sturdy box, such as a liquor-bottle box or shoe box
- 2 small mirrors of the same size
- a block of styrofoam
- black paper or black marker
- colored construction paper
- scissors
- glue
- masking tape

Directions

1. First, cut off the top and bottom of the liquor-bottle box (if you use a shoe box, tape the lid closed before cutting). Then cut two holes at opposite ends of the box (A). The holes should be the same size as the mirrors.
2. Next, use black paper (or a black marker) to completely cover (or darken) the inside of the box. Don't cover the holes if you use black paper. Decorate the outside by gluing colored construction paper around it.
3. Cut two triangular wedges out of the styrofoam. The wedges should fit into the corners of the box. Glue a mirror onto the widest side of each (B).
4. Now glue each triangle into a corner of the box, opposite each hole you cut (C).
5. Hold the periscope vertically, look into the bottom hole, and you'll be able to see out the top!

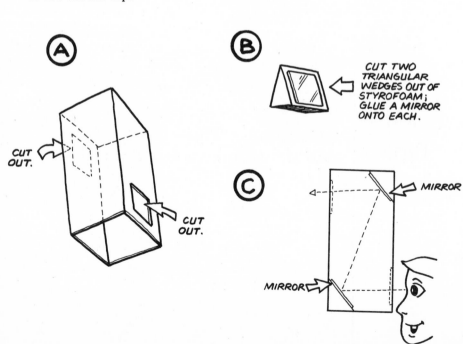

Getting Antsy!

You don't need to send away for an ant farm—you can make your very own in just a few simple steps.

What You'll Need

- a large glass jar (like a peanut butter jar)
- a small glass jar (like a jelly or applesauce jar)
- any size jar (to catch ants)
- soil
- sugar
- an eyedropper
- a drinking glass
- a wooden spoon
- sand
- water
- a plastic tub

Directions

1. It's best to do this project outside so that your parents won't have to worry about ants in the house! First, mix equal parts of soil and sand in a plastic tub.
2. Take the small jar and place it upside down inside the large jar (A).
3. Now you've got to catch some ants! Fill the third jar halfway with the soil and sand mixture. Then mix a little sugar and water together in the drinking glass and stir it into the soil and sand. Lay the jar on its side. The ants will be attracted to the sugar.
4. When enough ants have crawled into the jar, pour the ants and soil into the large jar. The mixture will surround the small jar. The narrow field of vision between the large and small jars will give you a good view of the ant tunnels (B). Add more soil and sand from the tub to fill up the jar.
5. Put the lid on the large jar tightly. You don't need to poke holes in the lid. Watch the ants build their own little colony right inside the jar! Once a week, open the jar and throw in a few bread crumbs or other food scraps. Add some drops of sugar water too, using the eyedropper.

One Step Further

Instead of ants, why not try pillbugs, earthworms (the soil must be kept damp), or any kind of ground beetle? Large glass jars also make great homes for caterpillars, spiders, and other creepy crawlies!

The World "Accordion" to You

It looks only like a cutout of your house but . . . presto! It opens up to reveal your family tree!

What You'll Need

- several feet of compu-ter paper (standard 8½" x 11" sheets)
- colored construction paper

- two pieces of card-board, 10" wide and 13" tall
- markers and crayons

- glue
- scissors

Directions

1. First, tear off a set of 10 sheets of computer paper. Do not tear off each individual sheet of paper. Now trace your family tree by asking your oldest relatives about their relatives and how they came to America or to the city you grew up in (A). Write the names of your earliest ancestors on the top sheet of computer paper. Then work your way down to the present. Make sure the bottom sheet is blank. If you don't need all 10 sheets, just tear off all but one of them.

2. Once that's done, you're ready to make the "house." Draw the shape of your house on the piece of cardboard. Use up as much of the cardboard as you can.

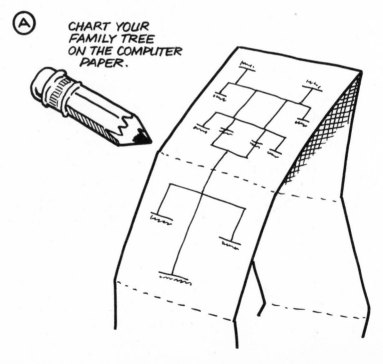

Ⓐ CHART YOUR FAMILY TREE ON THE COMPUTER PAPER.

3. Cut the shape out and put it on the second piece of cardboard. Trace around the shape, then cut the second piece of cardboard out. The two pieces will be the front and back of your house.
4. Decorate the front of your house using the colored construction paper, markers, and crayons.
5. Now decorate the back of your house, but make sure you work on the correct side, because when both decorated sides are facing outward, the shapes should mirror each other (B). When you're done, lay the back of the house colored side down, and place the front of the house over it, colored side up.
6. Take the computer paper with your family history and put it stacked between the front and back of your house. Glue the blank side of the top sheet to the inside of the front of your house. Then glue the blank bottom sheet to the inside of the back of your house. Let the glue dry overnight. When you pull the front and back sides of the house away from each other, it should open up like an accordion (C)!

THE DECORATED BOARDS SHOULD MIRROR EACH OTHER.

Cool Crayon Art

PARENTAL SUPERVISION REQUIRED
Turn ordinary crayons into a beautiful wall hanging that looks like stained glass.

What You'll Need

- crayons, assorted colors
- wax paper
- scissors
- a grater or pencil sharpener
- cardboard
- an old pillowcase
- an iron
- string

Directions

1. Tear off a large sheet of wax paper (about 2½ feet long) and lay it flat.
2. Next, make piles of crayon shavings using the grater or pencil sharpener. Spread the shavings all over the wax paper, distributing colors in whatever patterns you like. Don't put shavings near the edges.
3. Place another sheet of wax paper (the same size as the first one) over the shavings. Cover with an old pillowcase to protect the wax paper(A).
4. Now iron over the entire area of the paper. Ask an adult to help you out.
5. To make the borders for your wall hanging, cut two cardboard strips. Each should be as long as the wax paper and about 2" wide. Fold the strips in half the long way.
6. Place one cardboard strip over the top end of your wall hanging so that the flaps hang over each side of the wax paper. Glue each flap down. Then glue the second strip onto the bottom of the wall hanging (B).
7. Finally, punch a hole in the top border and put a string through it. Hang your art near a window so the light can shine through!

Ⓐ COVER THE WAX PAPER WITH AN OLD PILLOW-CASE BEFORE IRONING.

Ⓑ GLUE THE CARDBOARD FLAPS OVER THE WAX PAPER.

PUNCH A HOLE IN THE TOP; PUT A STRING THROUGH IT AND HANG.

Rolling Coasters

PARENTAL SUPERVISION RECOMMENDED
In just a few simple steps, you can make the coolest coasters this side of an amusement park!

What You'll Need

- lids from margarine, cottage cheese, or yogurt containers
- old greeting cards
- glue
- scissors
- a pencil
- spray shellac

Directions

1. If you'd like to make a set of coasters, they should all be the same size. Start by putting a lid on top of a greeting card illustration and tracing the lid shape onto the card. Make sure you get a portion of the illustration that will look good on your coaster! Pick the prettiest or funniest part of the card.
2. Cut out the circle. Glue the circle onto the top side of the lid. Repeat with as many lids as you like. Let them dry.
3. Take the lids outside and spray them with three coats of shellac. This will make your coasters waterproof in case any drinks spill on them. Make different sets of coasters to give as gifts!

One Step Further

What else can you use besides greeting cards? How about old photos, comics, colorful magazine ads, old wallpaper, scraps of fabric, cut-up book jackets, wrapping paper—just put your mind to it! Try natural items too, such as whole herbs or dried leaves from your backyard. You can just cut or break them to fit onto the lids. As long as you shellac the coasters, they'll be protected!

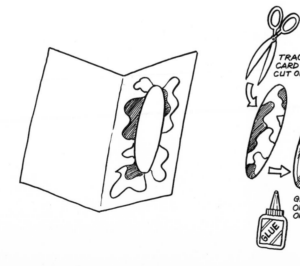

TRACE LID ON CARD AND CUT OUT.

GLUE CIRCLE ON TOP OF LID.

Using Your Noodle

Here's a nifty way to "pasta" time—making cool, colorful jewelry out of all those great macaroni and pasta shapes!

What You'll Need

- an assortment of dried pasta with holes, such as macaroni, wagon wheels, penne, mostaccioli, and rigatoni
- string or heavy thread
- craft paints, various colors
- scissors
- a paintbrush

Directions

1. First, gather an assortment of different pasta shapes. Before you start stringing, figure out how long you'd like your piece of jewelry to be by measuring the string around your neck, wrist, ankle, and so forth.
2. Now start threading the pasta shapes in any order you like. When you're done, tie the two ends of the string into a big knot.
3. Try it again, only this time use craft paints to paint the pasta all different colors before you string them! Give them as gifts to your friends and family.

One Step Further

Mix in other colorful objects with the pasta shapes, such as buttons and various sizes of beads, both plastic and glass. These add nice variety to your pasta jewelry. Make "drops" on a necklace by stringing two or three shapes on a short piece of string and then tying it to the necklace so that it hangs down.

Eggs-ceptional!

These little egg people are so much fun to make, you'll want to create your own eggs-clusive population!

What You'll Need

- eggs
- colored construction paper
- scissors
- lace or doilies

- yarn
- fabric scraps
- any small decorative items, such as flowers, bows, and sequins
- a bowl

- tape
- glue
- felt
- crayons
- a needle

Directions

1. See the Walking on Eggshells craft (p. 3) to find out how to blow out the insides of the eggs.
2. Now give your egg people character! Cut out felt or construction paper to make eyes and noses. Use the crayons or markers to add details. Add moustaches, freckles, or goatees! For hair, glue on strands of colored yarn.
3. To make a hat, cut a circle out of light cardboard or construction paper. Turn it into a cone shape by cutting a narrow triangle out of the circle and bringing the edges together. Decorate the hat by cutting a piece of fabric to fit over the cone shape. Glue the fabric on, then glue lace over the fabric or cut a doily to fit.
4. Finally, make a stand for your egg person by cutting a strip of construction paper about 4″ long and 1″ high. Glue the ends together to form a circle. Rest the egg on top. Put a little bow tie or flower on the stand, or color in a tie or collar!

Candle, Candle, Burning Bright

PARENTAL SUPERVISION RECOMMENDED
Light up the night (or day!) with your own colorful homemade candles. This project can get messy, so be careful when you're handling the hot wax!

What You'll Need

- one pound of paraffin (available at hardware stores)
- crayons, various colors
- 3 milk or juice cartons
- string
- 3 pencils
- newspaper
- 2 tin cans, one larger than the other
- scissors
- oven mitts

Directions

1. The cartons will serve as your candle molds. Start by cutting the tops off the cartons so you have three different heights. Put newspaper under the cartons to catch any wax drippings (A).
2. Cut three pieces of string, each a few inches longer than the height of each carton. These will be your wicks.
3. Next, tie a string around the middle of a pencil. Rest the pencil on top of the carton so that the string hangs down inside the center of it (B).
4. Now take the larger tin can and fill it halfway with tap water. Set the can on the stove on low heat.
5. Cut off a chunk of paraffin (about ¼ of the whole block) and put it into the smaller can. Now set the smaller can inside the larger can of water. If water starts getting into the smaller can, tip out some of the water.
6. Immediately put a crayon, any color, into the smaller can. The crayon will melt and color the wax.

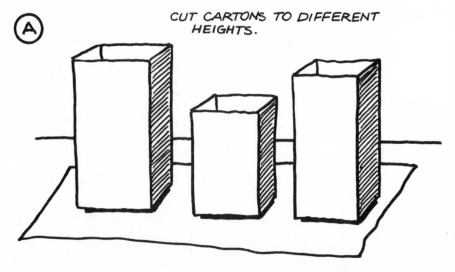

Ⓐ CUT CARTONS TO DIFFERENT HEIGHTS.

7. Once the paraffin and crayon have melted, turn off the stove. Now put on an oven mitt because the can is going to be hot! Carefully take out the smaller can and slowly pour the melted wax into one of the milk cartons (C). Stop at about 1" from the top of the carton.
8. Now be patient, because you have to let the wax cool completely. Don't move or touch the carton. When the wax has hardened, tear and peel off the milk carton. Cut the string near the pencil and remove the pencil, leaving the wick behind.
9. Repeat steps 3 through 8 for the other cartons you have—but this time use different colored crayons!

One Step Further

Try making a candle with different colored layers. Follow the steps above, but use a smaller chunk of paraffin. When you pour out the melted crayon and paraffin, fill the milk carton one-third of the way. Then repeat with another small chunk of paraffin and a different colored crayon. Continue with a variety of colors till the top layer is 1" from the top of the carton. Do red and green for a Christmas candle. Or try pink, red, and purple for a Valentine's Day gift. How about black and orange for Halloween?

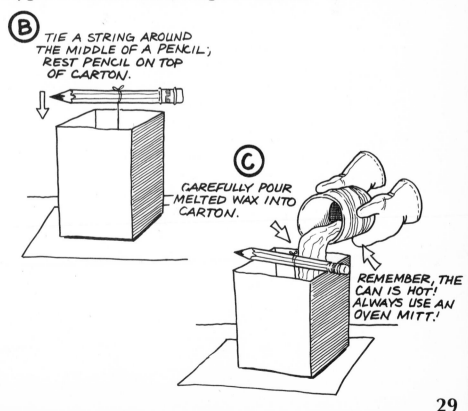

Ⓑ TIE A STRING AROUND THE MIDDLE OF A PENCIL; REST PENCIL ON TOP OF CARTON.

Ⓒ CAREFULLY POUR MELTED WAX INTO CARTON.

REMEMBER, THE CAN IS HOT! ALWAYS USE AN OVEN MITT!

Which Witch?

Learn how to transform an ordinary empty bottle into a spooky witch!

What You'll Need

- an empty glass bottle
- a nylon stocking
- needle and thread
- orange yarn and black yarn
- cotton balls
- black tissue or crepe paper
- black construction paper
- a pencil
- 2 black buttons
- glue
- masking tape
- scissors
- a ruler

Directions

1. To make the head, stuff a couple of handfuls of cotton balls into the foot of the stocking. Thread the needle and tie a knot at the end. You're going to make the witch's nose. Pinch the stocking between your thumb and forefinger, grabbing a wad of cotton underneath. Sew around the base of the nose, making a circle. Keep pinching the stocking and cotton while you're doing this.
2. When you're through, pull the needle and thread to tighten the stitches. The cotton will bunch up in the circle you made and stick out to form a nose. Stuff more cotton into the nose if you want. Secure your stitches by going over a previous stitch several times, making very tiny, tight stitches. Then cut off the thread.
3. Now sew on buttons for the eyes and yarn for the hair. Tie a knot in the stocking to hold the cotton in. Put the stocking into the mouth of the bottle so that the head rests on top. Tape the head down with masking tape.
4. Cover the witch's body by cutting a piece of tissue paper that will fit around the bottle. Fasten the paper to the bottle with a few drops of glue.

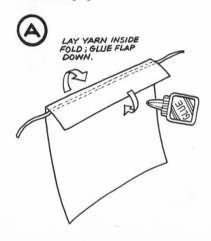

Ⓐ LAY YARN INSIDE FOLD ; GLUE FLAP DOWN.

5. To make the cloak, cut a 12″ x 10″ piece of tissue or crepe paper. Lay the paper horizontally and fold the top edge down to make a 2″ flap. Cut an 18″ piece of black yarn and lay it inside the fold along the crease. Then glue down the flap (A). Now put the cloak around the bottle and tie the ends of the yarn together in front.
6. Don't forget the hat! Cut a 12″ circle and a 4″ circle out of black construction paper. Cut a narrow triangle out of the larger circle. Bring the edges together to form a cone. Glue the cone to the smaller circle (B).
7. Finally, add hands and feet by cutting them out of black construction paper. Glue the hands on the front of the cloak. Attach the feet to the bottom of the glass.

One Step Further

Here's another doll you can make. Peel an apple and carve out a simple face on one side. Stick the pointed end of a pencil into the bottom of the apple. Put the other end of the pencil into the mouth of a bottle so that the apple rests on top. Decorate the bottle by papier-mâchéing it and painting it. Then let the apple dry and watch it turn into the face of an old person. Be patient—it can take up to a month!

(B) CUT OUT A 12″ CIRCLE AND A 4″ CIRCLE.

CUT A NARROW TRIANGLE OUT OF LARGER CIRCLE...

FORM A CONE...

THEN GLUE CONE TO 4″ CIRCLE.

(C)

Magic Mosaic

Everyday items take on a whole new meaning when you mix them in a mosaic!

What You'll Need

- a large piece of cardboard, 2 feet square
- a pencil
- toothpicks
- glue
- scissors
- string
- small, colorful, textured items such as broken eggshells, macaroni, rice, dried beans, dried peas, seashells, blades of grass, dried flowers, popcorn kernels, leaves, walnut shells, sunflower seeds, sequins, beads, cut-up drinking straws

Directions

1. On the cardboard, draw a big picture using the pencil. This will be the outline for your mosaic. It can be a scene, an animal, a self-portrait—use your imagination.
2. Use dabs of glue to fasten toothpicks onto your pencil lines (A). You may need to bend or break the toothpicks for the short or curved lines.
3. Pick one item, such as sunflower seeds, and fill one section by gluing them down. Try to fill the entire space so no cardboard shows through.
4. Now choose another item, one with a different color and texture, and fill the section next to the one you just filled.
5. Repeat until all the sections are covered. It should look like a patchwork quilt! Let your mosaic dry overnight, then shake it gently to get rid of any loose pieces.
6. Use scissors to punch a hole in the two upper corners of the cardboard. Thread a 2½-foot piece of string through one hole, across the back of the mosaic, and out the other hole. Bring the two ends together and tie a knot at the top. Now your mosaic is ready to hang (B)!

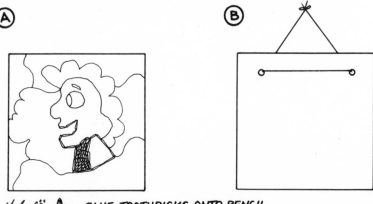

GLUE TOOTHPICKS ONTO PENCIL OUTLINES; THEN FILL SECTIONS WITH RICE, MACARONI, OR BEANS.

Fan-tastic!

This handmade fan is perfect for a hot summer day!

What You'll Need

- about 20 popsicle sticks (available at craft stores)
- light cardboard
- crayons, markers, or tempera paints, various colors
- masking tape
- a pencil
- scissors
- glue

Directions

1. First, cut the cardboard to make the front and back pieces of your fan. They should be the same size and shape, and the shape can be anything you want. The fan should be about 9″ wide. Cut a semicircle out of the bottom of each piece.
2. Draw a design on one side of the front piece. Do the same with the back piece.
3. To make the "ribs," lay a popsicle stick flat and put some glue on one end. Then lay the end of another popsicle stick over the glue and press the sticks together (A). You've made one rib. Repeat until you have three ribs.
4. Lay the front piece of your fan flat, colored side down. Glue the ribs onto the plain side, bringing the three ends together to form a point as shown. Then glue one popsicle stick to each corner, bringing their ends to a point as well (B). Let the glue dry.
5. Pick up the back piece of the fan and glue it onto the front piece, matching up the edges. The two plain sides should be facing each other. Let the glue dry.
6. Next, make the handle by laying five popsicle sticks flat. Put a piece of masking tape across the top and the bottom. This is one half of your handle. Repeat using five more sticks and two more strips of tape.
7. Take one half of the handle and turn it over so that the tape is on the bottom. Now glue the ends of the fan ribs onto the handle.

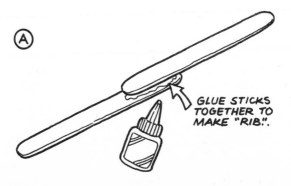

Ⓐ

GLUE STICKS TOGETHER TO MAKE "RIB".

8. Take a single popsicle stick and break off a 2″ piece. Glue this piece across the bottom of the handle half (C). Let dry.
9. Now take the other half of the handle and glue it, masking-tape side up, onto the first half (C). The fan ribs should be sandwiched between the two halves.
10. When the glue dries, wrap masking tape around the handle from top to bottom. Paint the handle.

One Step Further

You can decorate your fan in various fun ways. Try gluing on lace, sequins, glitter, feathers, old jewelry, fabric scraps, pieces of pretty gift wrap . . . use your imagination! You can also make a longer handle by gluing sticks end to end, like you did to make the ribs.

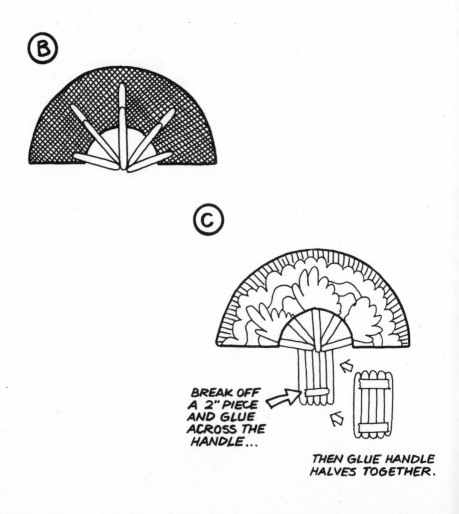

BREAK OFF
A 2″ PIECE
AND GLUE
ACROSS THE
HANDLE...

THEN GLUE HANDLE
HALVES TOGETHER.

Newspaper Hammock

Instead of recycling old newspapers, why not turn them into a hammock? Here's how.

What You'll Need

- lots of newspapers
- rope or strong clothesline
- tape
- scissors
- an old bedsheet

Directions

1. Make a stack of 30 sheets of newspaper. Roll up the stack the long way to form a tight, narrow tube. Tape the tube closed.
2. Repeat step 1 until you have about 20 tubes.
3. Cut three lengths of rope or clothesline, each at least 12 feet long. Lay the ropes parallel to one another.
4. Now tie each tube, one by one, to the ropes. Tie over-and-under knots, leaving 2″ to 3″ between each tube (A). Remember to leave at least 3 feet at the end of each rope so you can hang up the hammock.
5. When the hammock is long enough for you to lie in, tie the ropes together at each end (B). Hang your hammock between two trees in your backyard, or ask your mom or dad to help you hang it from your patio roof! Throw an old bedsheet over the hammock so you won't get newsprint on your clothes.

One Step Further

Try making a hammock out of brown shopping bags. Cut the bottom off each, then cut along a side seam and spread open the bag. Stack several bags, then roll them up.

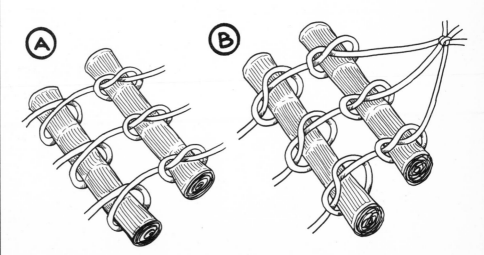

Terrific Totems

You only need a few items to make these colorful totem poles!

- empty toilet paper tubes
- crayons or markers
- colored construction paper (light colors work best)
- glue
- scissors

1. To start, cut a piece of construction paper large enough to wrap around a toilet paper tube.
2. Lay the paper flat and use the crayons or markers to draw a colorful totem face. Remember to start drawing the face in the middle of the paper. Leave space for the three-dimensional nose.
3. When you're done, wrap your totem face around the paper tube and secure it in the back with glue.
4. Now cut a nose out of construction paper. You can color the nose or just keep it the color of the construction paper. Make a crease down the middle of the nose and glue the edges onto your totem pole as shown. Pinch the nose along the crease to make it stick out.
5. Finally, cut a pair of wings out of construction paper and color them. Be sure to make the inner edge of each wing flat. Now glue the wings onto the totem pole. Make a whole set of funny or scary totems!

Try stacking your totem poles one on top of the other for a different effect. You can also use paper towel tubes instead of toilet paper tubes for bigger totems!

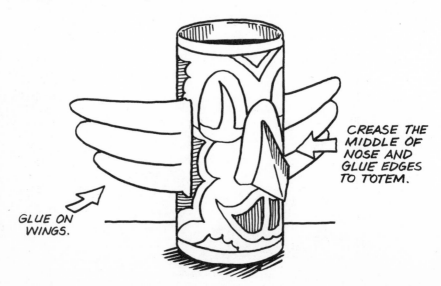

CREASE THE MIDDLE OF NOSE AND GLUE EDGES TO TOTEM.

GLUE ON WINGS.

You Scratch My Back . . .

For a quick and crazy craft, try this nifty crayon scratch art.

What You'll Need

- cardboard from a dress shirt package
- various crayons, including several black crayons
- objects such as paper clips, a ball-point pen, a fork, a comb, scissors, a compass point, a safety pin, a coin, and a spoon

Directions

1. Start by drawing all over the *entire* surface of the cardboard using the crayons. Use as many colors as you like, but save the black crayons for later. The more colors you use, the better.
2. Now cover your crayon drawing with black crayon (A). Press hard! Again, cover the entire surface. Make sure you have enough black crayons!
3. Next, take the sharp objects and scratch a picture out of the black crayon (B). Scratch out a picture of your house, your pet, a castle—anything you like. Be sure to scratch just hard enough to take the black off without removing the colored crayon underneath. Use a variety of objects. A paper clip makes a thin line, while the edge of a spoon makes a wider line. Don't remove all the black crayon, though—it helps make the assortment of colors underneath shine through!

One Step Further

Here's a similar art project called "crayon resist." Draw a picture on a piece of white paper and color it with crayons, but leave some white areas showing. Then lightly paint black watercolor over the picture. The crayon marks will "resist" the watercolor, and the paint will stay on the white areas of the paper, giving you a nice mix of paint and crayon.

Ⓐ   Ⓑ

Bag It!

Here's how to turn an old pair of blue jeans into a cool-looking purse, gym bag, or beach bag!

What You'll Need

- an old pair of blue jeans
- needle and thread
- heavy scissors

Directions

1. Start by cutting off the legs of the jeans about an inch below the fly. Save the legs to make into a strap.
2. If you've never sewn before, ask a parent or older brother or sister to help you out. But it's very easy. Cut a long piece of thread about the length of your arms outspread. Then thread it through the needle and tie a knot.
3. Bring together the front and back of the jeans at the bottom and sew it closed (A). Make small, tight stitches. You should go back and forth over your stitches at least twice to reinforce the bottom.
4. Next, you'll need to make a clasp to hold the top of the bag closed. Cut off the front button above the fly. Move the button to the back waistline and sew the button on the inside as shown (B). Now to close the bag, just push the newly sewn button through the original buttonhole!
5. To make the strap, fold one of the pants legs in half the long way and sew it closed.
6. Now sew each end of the strap to the inside of the waistline (C). Sew the strap securely, otherwise it may break when your bag is full. Now you're a real blue-jean baby!

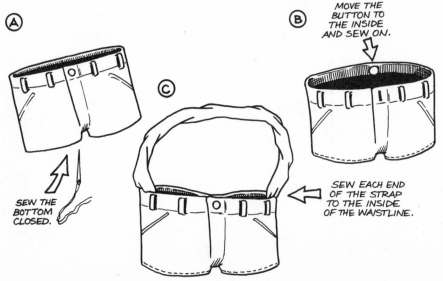

(A) SEW THE BOTTOM CLOSED.

(B) MOVE THE BUTTON TO THE INSIDE AND SEW ON.

(C) SEW EACH END OF THE STRAP TO THE INSIDE OF THE WAISTLINE.

Lights, Camera . . .

Follow these simple steps to become an amateur film projectionist!

What You'll Need

- clear acetate (available at art-supply stores)
- a half-gallon milk carton
- markers, various colors
- scissors
- a flashlight
- tape
- a ruler

Directions

1. Begin by washing and drying the milk carton thoroughly. Cut off the top and the bottom so that you have a rectangular tube for your "viewer."
2. Next, cut two slits, each about 3" high, on opposite sides of the carton (A).
3. Now cut strips of acetate, each just under 3" wide. Tape them together into one long "filmstrip."
4. Use a marker to divide the acetate strip into a series of frames, each about 3½" wide. Now, leaving the first frame empty, draw scenes on the frames using different colored markers. The scenes should tell a story.
5. Slide your "filmstrip" through one slit in the carton and out the other so that the first scene is inside the carton.
6. Turn off the lights. Shine the flashlight through an open end of the carton and onto a blank wall (B). The images you drew will be projected onto the wall. Pull the acetate through, frame by frame, until your "movie" is over!

One Step Further

Add color and character to your film projector by covering it with construction paper. Or papier-mâché it and then paint it. Add the name of your favorite movie theater. Make miniature projectors with pint-size cartons or quart-size cartons.

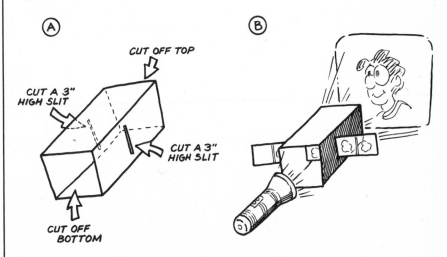

Ⓐ CUT OFF TOP
CUT A 3" HIGH SLIT
CUT A 3" HIGH SLIT
CUT OFF BOTTOM

Ⓑ

Shake It Up!

In just a snap, you can make a snazzy snow-dome paperweight like those you see in souvenir shops!

What You'll Need

- an empty baby food jar
- a small amount of rubber cement
- a small plastic flower and stem
- a teaspoon
- silver glitter
- water
- glue

Directions

1. First, clean out the baby food jar. Wash the label off.
2. Hold the flower next to the jar. If it's taller than the jar, cut the stem to fit.
3. Next, take the lid and turn it upside down so that the inside part is facing up. Put the lid on the table and put a drop or two of cement in the center of the lid.
4. Attach the flower by sticking its stem in the cement (A). Hold the flower for a few minutes until the cement hardens. If the flower is not secure, add another drop or two of cement and let it dry.
5. Now fill the jar with water until the water is about ¼" from the top. Put two teaspoons of the glitter into the water for the "snow."
6. Put glue around the inside edge of the lid, and put a few drops of glue around the rim of the jar, too (B). Screw the lid on. Make sure the jar is upright (the flower will be hanging upside down), and let the glue dry.
7. Turn the jar so the flower is upright. Shake, shake, shake!

One Step Further

Substitute small plastic figures for the plastic flower. Make sure they fit in the jar, though. Put in sequins instead of glitter, or combine the two! Use a jelly jar or other glass jar—then you can use larger plastic figures and add twice as much "snow"!

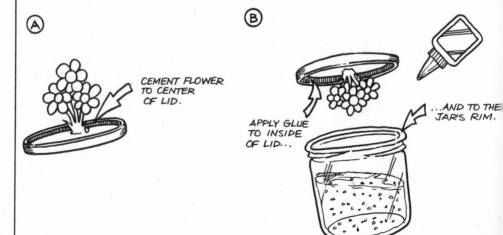

Ⓐ CEMENT FLOWER TO CENTER OF LID.

Ⓑ APPLY GLUE TO INSIDE OF LID... ...AND TO THE JAR'S RIM.

Paper Perfect

PARENTAL SUPERVISION RECOMMENDED

Did you know that you can actually make a sheet of paper right in your own home? Here's how!

What You'll Need

- 30 sheets of regular facial tissue
- a baking pan, baking dish, or tub (about 8" x 10" large and 2" deep)
- an iron

- a large mixing bowl
- a measuring cup
- a piece of wire window screen, small enough to fit in the pan, dish, or tub

- an eggbeater
- liquid laundry starch
- newspaper
- a clean rag

Directions

1. Before you begin, lay down at least a dozen sheets of newspaper. These will serve as your blotters.
2. First, you'll need to make the pulp. Fill the bowl halfway with hot water (but not too hot to touch). Shred the tissues into small pieces and put them in the water. Put your fingers in the water and shred the tissues further until they dissolve. The pulp will look like thin breakfast cereal.
3. Mix in two ounces of starch to help strengthen the paper.
4. Now pour the pulp into the baking pan, dish, or tub. Add enough water to raise the level to at least 1" from the bottom of the pan. Stir vigorously using the eggbeater.
5. Next, slide the screen into the water, then slowly pull it out using both hands. Some of the pulp will be carried out with the screen. Hold the screen over the pan to drain the excess water and gently shake the screen to distribute the pulp evenly (A).
6. When almost all the water has drained off, lay the screen on the newspapers. Let the pulp dry until it is damp.
7. While the paper is still damp, peel it off the screen. Put a clean rag over the paper and press it with a warm iron (B). This will compress the fibers and strengthen the paper. You should be able to make four to six sheets of paper with each batch of your "paper recipe."

One Step Further

Substitute newspapers or typing paper for the facial tissues. Try adding a few drops of enamel oil paints for color. Take sheets of notebook paper, put them between two sheets of your homemade paper, and bind them together to make a diary or journal!

Ⓐ

GENTLY SHAKE SCREEN TO EVENLY DISTRIBUTE THE PULP.

Ⓑ

PLACE A CLEAN RAG OVER PAPER AND IRON.

Carton Critters

The steps below will show you how to make a chick out of an egg carton, but after that, think of some critters to make on your own!

What You'll Need

- a cardboard egg carton
- tempera paints, various colors
- buttons, feathers, sequins, colored tissue paper
- scissors
- glue

Directions

1. To make the head, cut off an end pair of cones from the egg carton. On one side of each cone you will see a pointed piece. This is the chick's beak. Hold onto this piece and trim off about ¾" around the edge of the cone. Don't cut off the beak!
2. Fold out the beak on each cone so that it sticks out. Put glue around the edge of one cone. Turn the other cone upside down and press it down on top of the first cone, matching up the beak pieces (A). Let the glue dry, then trim the beak a little.
3. Now it's time to make the chick's body. Cut off another pair of cones (not the other end pair). Each of these cones will have two points sticking up. Hold onto the points of one cone and trim off about ¾" around the edge (don't cut off the points—they're your chick's wings). Take the other cone and do the same, but this time cut off its two points.
4. Fold out the two points on the first cone to make them stick out. Then take the second cone and glue it on top of the other cone (B).
5. Now glue the head onto the body. Let it dry.
6. Paint the chick yellow with an orange beak. Glue on buttons for eyes and feathers for its tail. Add sequins and pieces of tissue paper to make it bright and cheerful!

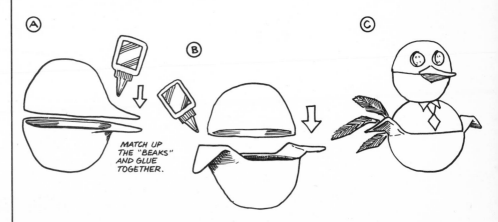

MATCH UP THE "BEAKS" AND GLUE TOGETHER.

This One's for the Birds!

Have fun watching your fine feathered friends by creating these simple but effective bird feeders using ordinary household objects! You can buy birdseed at any grocery or pet supply store.

Directions

Bleach Bottle Feeder

For this feeder, cut four 3" x 3" windows out of the sides of an empty, rinsed bleach bottle. The windows should start 1" from the bottom of the container. Sand down the rough edges with sandpaper or cover the edges with black electrical tape. Next, use a hammer and large nail to poke a hole in the middle of the bottle cap. Cut a 12" piece of string and tie the two ends together. Then thread the looped end through the hole and tie a big knot so the string won't slip through the hole. Now you've got a big loop to hang the bottle feeder from a tree branch or a nail in your roof.

BLEACH BOTTLE
FEEDER

PLASTIC BOTTLE
FEEDER

Plastic Bottle Feeder

Cut a 3" x 4" window out of an empty 2-liter plastic bottle. The window should be about 2" from the bottom of the bottle. Sand down the edges or tape over them. Now take an empty pie tin and glue it to the bottom of the plastic bottle. To hang up this bird feeder, follow the directions for the Bleach Bottle Feeder.

Orange Bag Feeder

The mesh bag of oranges you buy at the grocery store makes an ideal bird feeder. Just fill the empty bag half full with birdseed and tie a knot at the top of the bag. Use the point of a scissors to poke a hole through the bag underneath the knot. Put string through the hole, tie both ends at the top, and it's ready to hang!

ORANGE BAG
FEEDER

Pine Cone Feeder

Pick up a pine cone or two next time you're walking through your neighborhood or a park. Mix together half a jar of peanut butter, a handful of birdseed, and a handful of uncooked oatmeal in a bowl till the mixture is gooey and sticky. With a butter knife, smear the mixture all over the pine cone. Tie a string around the top for hanging.

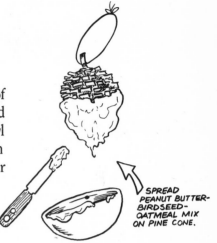

SPREAD PEANUT BUTTER-BIRDSEED-OATMEAL MIX ON PINE CONE.

PINE CONE FEEDER

Doughnut Feeder

You only need a doughnut, 2 jar lids, some string, and a hammer and nail to make this fun feeder! Use the hammer and nail to make a small hole in the center of each lid. Cut a 12" piece of string. Thread the string through one lid, then through the doughnut hole, then through the other lid. Tie a knot under the bottom lid. Tie the other end of the string onto a tree branch and let it hang (the lids and the doughnut will touch each other). Watch the birds flock to your new feeder!

DOUGHNUT FEEDER

PUT STRING THROUGH SLATS.

NEST HELPER

One Step Further

Try making a Nest Helper. Find a pants hanger that has a cardboard tube around the bottom. With a hobby knife, cut a row of slats on both sides of the tube. Stuff strands of thread or light string into the slats so that they hang down. Put the hanger on a branch and watch the birds take the thread to build their nests!

45

What a Relief!

You can have a ball molding homemade dough into a nifty relief map—and learn a little about geography at the same time!

What You'll Need

- 3 cups of flour
- 1 cup of salt
- 3 tablespoons dry wheat paste powder
- 1¼ cups lukewarm water
- an 11″ x 17″ piece of cardboard
- an 11″ x 17″ piece of white construction paper
- a large mixing bowl
- craft paints, various colors
- encyclopedia or atlas
- glue
- a frying pan
- a pencil
- an atlas
- paintbrushes
- a wooden spoon

Directions

1. Begin by drawing the shape of the United States on the white construction paper. Use an atlas as a guide. Glue the paper onto the cardboard.
2. You need to make the dough next. Heat the salt in the pan over low heat for about 5 minutes. Then mix the salt, flour, and paste together in a bowl. Slowly add the lukewarm water as you continue to stir. If the mixture feels too dry, add water. Knead the dough till it's soft and pliable.
3. Then, still using the atlas as a guide, use chunks of dough to fill in your map! Do the mountain ranges first, starting with the Sierra Nevadas. Make some mountaintops low and ragged, others high and smooth. Fill in the rest of the map with dough, then let it dry.
4. Now paint the details! Put snow and trees on the mountaintops. Paint in all the lakes, rivers, and waterways. Paint each state a different color, and use a smaller brush to add the name of each state.

Soapy Sculptures

PARENTAL SUPERVISION REQUIRED
Learn how to turn a plain bar of soap into a "squeaky clean" sculpture!

What You'll Need

- a bar of soap, any kind
- a kitchen knife
- a pencil

Directions

1. First, use the pencil to draw the outline of an animal directly on the bar of soap. Take up as much of the bar as you can. Draw a bear, cat, fish, alligator, bird—any animal you'd like. Refer to a photo book of real animals to guide you.
2. Take the knife and carve around the outline you drew, cutting off the excess soap.
3. Now use the knife to carefully shape the animal and make it three-dimensional. Be careful not to cut yourself. You can sprinkle water on the soap to help you mold it easier. Water also gets rid of any mistakes you may make!
4. Cut small notches to show muscle definition. Try making cross-hatching marks to add texture. For example, if you're carving an alligator, a cross-hatching pattern on its back will make your 'gator look more real.

One Step Further

For variety, try different-colored soaps. Try making a lizard out of a bar of Irish Spring. Turn a pink cake of soap into a flamingo or white soap into a swan. Or try your hand at sculpting other objects such as seashells or mushrooms. To make your soapy creations more realistic, paint them with craft paints! (If you paint them, just use them for decoration—don't wash your hands with them!)

34

An Egg-citing Mobile

Colored eggshells are what give this fun mobile an egg-stra special look!

What You'll Need

- a dozen eggs
- construction paper, any color
- a small paintbrush
- craft paints, various colors

- a penny
- a pencil
- scissors
- needle and thread
- tissue or crepe paper, various colors

- a straight pin
- a wire hanger
- a small mixing bowl
- laundry starch
- a ruler

Directions

1. Follow the directions under Walking on Eggshells (p. 3) to blow out the insides of the eggs. Then cut or tear small strips of the tissue or crepe paper. Papier-mâché the eggshells and the wire hanger with bright colors (see It's a Piñata! on p. 13 for directions). You can also paint some of the eggshells with craft paints.
2. Trace the penny on the construction paper and cut it out. Cut a 16" piece of thread, double it up, and thread the needle, tying a big knot at the end of the thread.
3. Now poke the needle through the center of the circle. Slide the circle all the way down to the knot (A).
4. Choose an eggshell. Push the needle through the smaller hole. Shake the egg gently to make the needle come out the larger hole. Grab the needle and slide the eggshell down to the paper circle (A). Cut off the thread and tie it onto the bottom of the hanger so that the egg hangs down.
5. Repeat steps 2 through 5 for the remaining eggs, except cut alternating long and short pieces of thread so the eggs hang at varying lengths (B).

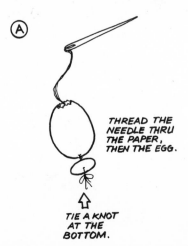

Ⓐ

THREAD THE
NEEDLE THRU
THE PAPER,
THEN THE EGG.

⇧
TIE A KNOT
AT THE
BOTTOM.

Ⓑ

Melted Plastic Ornaments

PARENTAL SUPERVISION REQUIRED
Here's a way to make cool ornaments right in your own kitchen!

What You'll Need

- plastic berry baskets
- small glass beads
- any plastic-coated wire (available at hardware stores)
- 3- or 4-quart saucepan
- aluminum pie pan
- needle and thread
- kitchen tongs
- scissors
- glue
- glitter

Directions

1. Fill the saucepan with water and heat it on the stove (but don't boil it). The water should be deep enough to completely cover the basket.
2. Drop the plastic basket into the hot water. When the basket has collapsed and changed shape, pull it out using the tongs. Put it on a pie pan to cool.
3. Now string some glass beads onto a 24" piece of coated wire. MAKE SURE TO CUT OFF ANY WIRE ENDS THAT ARE SHOWING. Weave the beads in and out of the holes in the basket. The wire will conform to the shape of the basket.
4. Put dabs of glue on various areas of the basket and sprinkle glitter over it.
5. To make a hanger, cut another piece of coated wire about 5" long. Weave it through one of the holes. Tie both ends together at the top.

One Step Further

Try dropping a plastic cup into the hot water. It will melt into a nifty bell shape. Use colored cups for variety. To make a hole for hanging, ask a parent to heat the point of a large sewing needle by holding a lit match to it for a few seconds. Then poke a hole in the plastic with the heated needle.

TO MAKE A HANGER, WEAVE A WIRE THROUGH AND TIE A KNOT.

WEAVE THE WIRED BEADS THROUGH THE BASKET.

49

Balloon Blast-Off!

Learn how to make a nifty balloon rocket that actually takes off! You'll need a friend to help you with this one.

What You'll Need

- fishing line
- plastic drinking straws
- balloons
- masking tape

Directions

1. Start by measuring out a piece of fishing line the length of your bedroom or living room.
2. Tie one end to a doorknob or a piece of heavy furniture at one end of the room.
3. Next, run the fishing line through a straw. Then stretch the line across the room and attach the other end to another doorknob or piece of furniture.
4. Blow up the balloon and pinch the end to hold in the air. Have your friend tape the top of the balloon to the straw so that the balloon hangs down.
5. Still holding the balloon closed, walk the straw and balloon to one end of the fishing line. Turn so that you are facing the opposite end of the fishing line.
6. Now start your countdown! When you reach zero, let go of the balloon. The escaping air will act as jet propulsion to push the balloon forward on the fishing line!

One Step Further

You can string more than one fishing line across the room and have a balloon-rocket race with your friends. Or you can use this method as an intercom to send secret messages to your brother or sister in another room. Just tape a note to the balloon and let 'er rip! Experiment a little. Get a parent to help you string fishing line from a roof or tree so your blast-off can be vertical!

Cotton Swab Art

Create a nifty double-sided piece of art using simple cotton swabs!

What You'll Need

- 3 to 4 large boxes of cotton swabs (wooden sticks work best)
- color markers
- craft paints, various colors
- a narrow paintbrush
- light cardboard
- scissors
- tape
- a ruler

- 2 pieces of plastic canvas, about 6½" x 6½", with 5 holes per inch (available in the needlepoint section at craft stores)

Directions

1. To start, push a cotton swab through a square in one piece of the plastic canvas. You're going to fill the whole canvas using the swabs.
2. Now line up the second piece of canvas with the first one. Push the swab through the second piece to "connect" the canvases.
3. Take another swab and poke it through each canvas next to the first swab. Continue doing this, filling up each row (A). When you're through, the two pieces of canvas should stand upright on their own.
4. Now turn one side of the canvas toward you. Think of an outdoor scene, a mosaic, whatever you like. Then start painting the tips of the swabs. Be careful not to make a mistake (it will be difficult to replace the swabs). When you're done, paint a different scene or design on the other side.
5. To make the frame, measure the space between the two pieces of canvas. Cut a strip of cardboard so that it is a little wider than that space. The strip should be long enough to wrap all the way around your artwork.
6. Color the frame using the paints or markers. Then wrap it around your cotton swab art and tape it at the bottom (B). Your masterpiece is done!

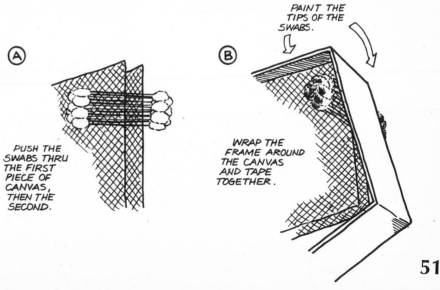

Ⓐ PUSH THE SWABS THRU THE FIRST PIECE OF CANVAS, THEN THE SECOND.

Ⓑ WRAP THE FRAME AROUND THE CANVAS AND TAPE TOGETHER.

PAINT THE TIPS OF THE SWABS.

A Really Big Shoe

Take a "step" in the right direction by turning an old shoe into a playful planter!

What You'll Need

- a big, old shoe (canvas works best, but leather is fine, too)
- a small indoor or outdoor plant (such as a cactus or African violet) that fits inside the shoe
- laundry starch
- newspaper
- a paintbrush
- tempera paints, various colors

Directions

1. Before you begin, lay down some sheets of newspaper on your work table.
2. Now put the shoe on the newspaper. If there are any shoelaces, remove them. Papier-mâché the entire shoe, following the instruction given in It's a Piñata! (p. 13). Do two layers of papier-mâché, allowing the first layer to dry before you apply the next.
3. Once the shoe is stiff and dry, paint it! Be creative. Make lightning bolts, symbols, or fake buckles and laces. Let the paint dry overnight.
4. Now, LEAVING THE PLANT IN ITS ORIGINAL POT, place it inside the shoe. Try this nifty craft again using a different kind of shoe—maybe a high-top or a penny loafer!

39

A Rose Is a Rose

Even a paper rose, by any other name, is still a beautiful rose.

What You'll Need

- red and green tissue paper
- a cup or bowl
- scissors
- wire stems and florist's tape (available at florist's shops)
- a glass bottle
- a pencil
- a stapler
- a ruler

Directions

1. First, cut 18 squares of red tissue paper. Each square should be 4" x 4".
2. Next, put the cup or bowl upside down on a stack of about four tissues and trace around it with the pencil. Cut out the circles. Repeat with another stack until you have 18 circles.
3. Then make a small loop at one end of a wire stem. Thread six circles onto the stem by poking the pointed end through the center of each circle. Bunch the circles loosely around the loop, then staple them once at the bottom (A).
4. Do the same with six more circles and staple them onto the others. Then repeat with the last six circles.
5. Now cut a long piece of florist's tape. With one hand, hold one end of the tape over the last staple. Use your other hand to wrap tape around the bottom of the flower about three or four times. Then continue winding tape down and around the stem.
6. Don't forget the leaves! Cut four 4" x 4" squares out of the green tissue paper. Now stack them and cut out a three-leaf shape. Tape the leaves onto the wire.
7. Finally, fluff out the rose layer by layer so it looks like it's in bloom (B). Put it into a small glass bottle that's been papier-mâchéd and painted and give it as a gift!

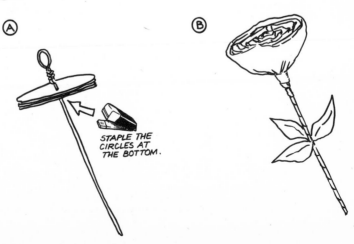

Ⓐ

STAPLE THE
CIRCLES AT
THE BOTTOM.

Ⓑ

Rolling in Dough

You'll be amazed at all the things you can do with this homemade dough. Just follow the simple recipe below.

What You'll Need

- 4 cups of flour
- 1 cup of salt
- 1½ cups of water
- a large mixing bowl
- a nonstick (or greased) disposable cookie sheet
- craft paints, various colors
- newspaper
- a wooden spoon
- a paintbrush
- spray lacquer

Directions

1. In the mixing bowl, combine the flour, salt, and water and mix well with the wooden spoon.
2. Mold the dough into different shapes, such as fruits, vegetables, animals, creepy insects, or miniature animals. Spread them out on the disposable cookie sheet and bake at 350 degrees for one hour.
3. Take out the dough and let it cool. Then paint the shapes.
4. When the paint is dry, take the figures outside and place them on sheets of newspaper. Spray them with lacquer to keep the paint from chipping.

One Step Further

You can make all sorts of crafts with this moldable dough. Glue a magnet on the back and stick it on the refrigerator. Make Christmas or Hanukkah ornaments. Just glue a piece of thread or string on the back of the ornament and it's ready to hang! You can also roll beads into different shapes, poke a nail through each to make a hole, and bake the beads. Then paint them, string them, and make necklaces and bracelets!

Make a Good Impression

Did you know that you can create interesting textures and patterns using simple household objects—including fruits and vegetables?

What You'll Need

- tempera paints, various colors
- apples, potatoes, starfruit, mushrooms
- a stack of computer paper
- several sponges
- empty spools, clothespins, buttons, corks, bottle caps
- 2 wooden dowels, at least 1" wider than the computer paper
- glue
- scissors
- string
- kitchen knife
- several empty milk cartons

Directions

1. First, prepare your printing tools. Slice a raw potato in half and carve a heart on the inside of one half. Then dig out the potato around the heart so that the heart sticks up. Leave the other half uncut. Do the same with the apple, except cut a different shape. Cut the starfruit in half. Cut some of the sponges into squares, circles, and triangles.
2. To make a stamp pad, cut a clean milk carton to about 3" high. Cut a sponge to fit, moisten it with water, and pour some paint on it. Do the same with another milk carton and a different color of paint.
3. Spread out several sheets of computer paper, but don't tear them apart.
4. Now go stamp crazy! Choose a printing tool, dip it in your stamp pad, and stamp it all over the paper (A). Repeat with a different tool (anything that will make an interesting shape or texture) and a different color. Make sure you have plenty of objects, because each can probably be used only once.
5. When you're finished, tear your artwork off at the top and bottom and let it dry. Then put glue on a wooden dowel and roll the top sheet around it twice. Take the second dowel and do the same with the bottom sheet.
6. Cut a piece of string about 2 feet long. Tie each end to opposite ends of the top dowel. Now your artwork is ready to hang (B)!

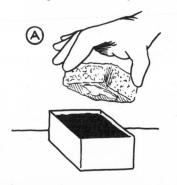

As Time Goes By

Dig out those mementos of yours and turn them into a great gift your mom or dad will treasure forever!

What You'll Need

- a large piece of cardboard, at least 16" by 20"
- crayons, markers, or paints (various colors)
- a paintbrush
- scissors
- glue

- award ribbons, certificates, report cards, tests, book reports, baby photos, your horoscope, your baby bracelet, school assembly programs, pictures you drew, a lock of your hair, and other mementos

Directions

1. Gather all your mementos in front of you. Take some of the bigger items—such as newspaper clippings and pictures you drew—and trim them into different shapes.
2. Start gluing the items on the cardboard one by one. You might want to arrange them loosely in some sort of design first, then glue them down. Or just put them down in a random pattern. Overlap the items so no cardboard shows through.
3. Now add artistic flair to your collage by swashing strokes of paint here and there, outlining some of the items in crayon, and underlining important things in marker.
4. Once your collage is finished, ask an adult to help you get it framed. You can buy the supplies to make a frame at an art store, or sometimes the art store will frame a picture for you. This collage makes a wonderful gift for your mom or dad. After all, you wouldn't be here if it weren't for them!

Rockin' Candy

PARENTAL SUPERVISION REQUIRED
In one week, you can grow your own rock candy mountain. See if you can wait that long to eat it!

What You'll Need

- 1 cup of water
- 4 cups of sugar
- piece of heavy cord (the length of the jar)

- 3- or 4-quart saucepan
- a large glass jar
- oven mitts
- scissors

- a wooden spoon
- a dinner plate
- a pencil

Directions

1. To begin, put the water and two cups of the sugar into the saucepan and heat over the stove, stirring with the wooden spoon until the sugar has dissolved.
2. Stir in the remaining two cups of sugar little by little. Continue heating until all the sugar has dissolved. Then pour all the liquid into the glass jar. BE SURE TO USE OVEN MITTS!
3. Now tie one end of the cord around the middle of the pencil. Balance the pencil over the mouth of the jar so that the cord hangs down into the liquid. In a few hours, sugar crystals will begin to form on the cord.
4. The next day, take out the cord and place it on a dinner plate. You'll notice that crystals have also formed on the sides of the jar. To get rid of these, pour the liquid out of the jar into the saucepan and reheat it.
5. When the liquid is hot (but not boiling), pour it back into the jar, using oven mitts. The liquid will dissolve the crystals on the sides of the jar. LET THE LIQUID COOL.
6. When the liquid is lukewarm, put the cord with the crystals back into the jar, resting the pencil over the mouth.
7. Repeat steps 4 through 6 every day for a week until you have a big rock candy mountain!

Paper Sculpture

PARENTAL SUPERVISION REQUIRED

Don't get this challenging craft confused with papier-mâché. Paper sculpture involves bending, scoring, and folding flat paper to make three-dimensional art! The steps below will show you how to make a paper-sculpture poodle.

What You'll Need

- heavy paper, such as drawing paper or construction paper
- a hobby knife or single-edged razor blade
- rubber cement or glue
- newspaper or thick cardboard
- notebook paper or typing paper
- a ruler
- a pencil
- scissors

Directions

1. Start with a sheet of heavy paper that is at least 12" x 8". Lay the paper horizontally. Put a stack of newspapers or a piece of thick cardboard underneath to protect your work surface.
2. Draw a side view of a dog. You only need to draw one front leg and one back leg, but make them wide, because you will be scoring and bending them to look like four legs (A). Try to use up most of the paper. Then cut out the dog.
3. To score his legs, lightly draw a slightly curved line to divide the front leg into two legs. Do the same to the back leg. Then, carefully run, or score, the back of the hobby knife or razor blade along the lines you drew (B). Press just hard enough to cut through the topmost layer of the paper. DON'T CUT THROUGH THE PAPER.

DRAW AND CUT OUT A SIDE VIEW OF A DOG.

SCORE THE LEGS, CHIN AND TAIL WITH THE BACK OF A HOBBY KNIFE.

4. Now gently fold the legs along the cuts you made so that the lines you scored stick up and are *outside* the fold, facing you (C). Score the tail and chin the same way.
5. Next, you'll need to make fringes for your poodle's head, body, legs, and tail. Cut several strips of the notebook paper or typing paper. Each strip should be at least 2″ wide. Vary the length depending on the size of the head, the tail, and so forth. Cut slits in each strip, then curl them by running them over the sharp edge of a scissors blade or a ruler (D).
6. Now attach each fringe of curls to your poodle using rubber cement or glue. Put each fringe right up against the other to create rows of curls. You can mount your paper sculpture by rubber-cementing it to a construction paper background of a contrasting color to make your art stand out (E).

One Step Further

You can create all sorts of things with paper sculpture—just put your mind to it! Use different-colored paper for variety. Cut semicircles and bend them out to make eyes, mouths, and other features. Once you know how to score the paper, you can create all sorts of three-dimensional effects. Just remember that the scored lines are always on the outside of the folds, so try scoring both sides of the paper and bending it both ways for that "3-D" look!

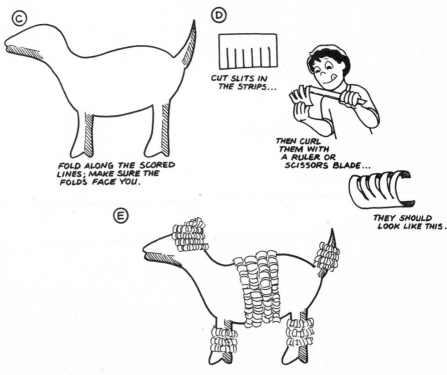

Ⓒ FOLD ALONG THE SCORED LINES; MAKE SURE THE FOLDS FACE YOU.

Ⓓ CUT SLITS IN THE STRIPS...

THEN CURL THEM WITH A RULER OR SCISSORS BLADE...

THEY SHOULD LOOK LIKE THIS.

Ⓔ

Magic Crystals

Use ordinary charcoal to grow colorful crystals right before your eyes!

What You'll Need

- charcoal briquettes
- a disposable shallow cooking pan
- food coloring, any color
- a paper cup
- a mixing spoon

- 3 tablespoons of salt
- 3 tablespoons of liquid bluing (available at grocery stores)
- 3 tablespoons of clear ammonia

Directions

1. Begin by spreading out enough charcoal briquettes to cover the bottom of the cooking pan.
2. Put a few drops of food coloring over the briquettes.
3. Mix the salt, bluing, and ammonia together in the paper cup and pour the solution over the charcoal. BE CAREFUL NOT TO SMELL THE AMMONIA DIRECTLY. In just a few hours, crystals will start to grow!
4. You need to coat the charcoals with the solution each day. Just repeat step 3 and pour the mixture over the briquettes to keep the crystals growing. When you think they've grown enough, stop applying the liquid.

One Step Further

Try using different colors of food coloring to create two-tone or three-tone crystals. See if you can make the crystals grow into various shapes by pouring the ammonia solution over certain areas to create a pattern.

ADD A FEW DROPS OF FOOD COLORING.

THEN ADD THE AMMONIA MIXTURE.

Bull-Roarer

PARENTAL SUPERVISION REQUIRED

According to folklore, when the Indians whirled bull-roarers over their heads, the whooshing sound resembled the wind blowing. The Indians used bull-roarers to summon rain.

What You'll Need

- a thin, flat piece of wood at least 6″ long
- a ruler
- sandpaper or a heavy file
- cord or string
- a drill
- scissors

Directions

1. Get your dad or another adult to help you make the bull-roarer. The piece of wood can be any rectangular or square shape, just as long as it's thin and flat. Taper two opposing sides using the file or sandpaper. Then file down one end to create a rounded shape. File it down till it's smooth.
2. Next, drill a hole in the opposite end near the edge. Cut a piece of cord or string, 3 to 4 feet long. Put one end through the hole and tie a tight knot.
3. Now test your bull-roarer! It's best not to do this in the house. Go outside and stand in an area where you won't hit anything or anyone. Whirl the bull-roarer over your head in a fast circular motion. Don't be surprised if the sound comes and goes; that's how the bull-roarer works.

One Step Further

You can paint bright colors and patterns on your bull-roarer. Try making a bull-roarer using an oval or circular piece of wood this time. Try different sizes of wood, too. See if there's any difference in the sound each one makes.

WHIRRRRR!

FILE DOWN SIDES AND ROUND OFF THE TOP.

I Spy Tie-Dye

PARENTAL SUPERVISION REQUIRED
The art of tie-dyeing is so simple and fun, no wonder it's still as popular today as it was during the sixties!

What You'll Need

- one-gallon empty bottle
- old clothes, such as T-shirts or shorts
- 3 plastic buckets
- rubber gloves or clothespin
- bleach
- an apron or smock
- string or rubber bands
- dye (Rit or Tintex), various colors
- newspaper
- old towels

Directions

For light-colored fabric, use dye. For dark-colored fabric, use bleach. Put on the apron or smock before you start.

1. To prepare the dye: Pour a package of dye powder, any color, into the gallon bottle and fill it with hot tap water. Put the top on and shake well. Pour the liquid into a plastic bucket. To prepare the bleach: Pour the bleach about 2" deep into another plastic bucket. Do this outside or near an open window. DON'T TOUCH THE BLEACH OR SMELL IT DIRECTLY! Fill the third bucket with plain water.

2. Now tie string or rubber bands around the fabric in as many places as you want (A).

3. ALWAYS WEAR GLOVES WHEN YOU'RE DIPPING FABRIC. If you don't have gloves, use a clothespin to pick up the fabric. Dip the fabric into the dye or bleach for 2 to 3 minutes (B). You can put the whole piece of fabric in, or just dip the parts that are tied. For light-colored fabrics, wait until the fabric is a little darker than you want it to be. For dark-colored fabrics, wait until it has turned as light as you want it to be.

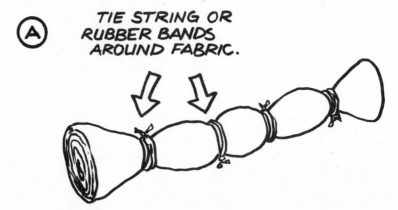

Ⓐ TIE STRING OR RUBBER BANDS AROUND FABRIC.

4. Pick up the fabric and swirl it in the bucket of plain water.
5. Wrap the fabric in some old towels and press down on it to soak up the water.
6. Take off the string or rubber bands and hang up the fabric to dry. Put newspapers below to catch any dripping water. You'll have a great piece of tie-dye overnight!

One Step Further

You can tie-dye the same shirt or piece of clothing in different colors. Get an extra bucket for each color. After the first dipping, rinse the fabric but don't remove the string or rubber bands. Then dip the fabric into a different-colored dye. Change the water in the bucket after each color. Try tie-dyeing old pillowcases or bedsheets!

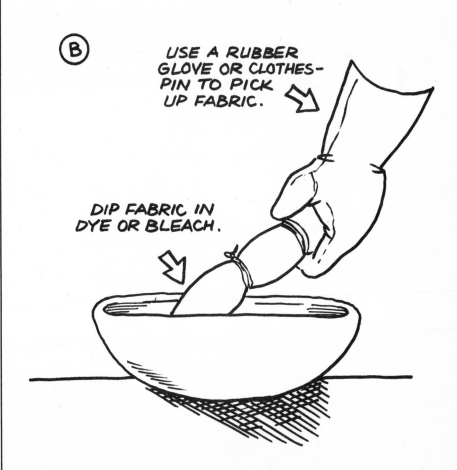

USE A RUBBER GLOVE OR CLOTHES-PIN TO PICK UP FABRIC.

DIP FABRIC IN DYE OR BLEACH.

48 Dancing Marionettes

Everybody loves puppets. Here's how to make your very own marionette!

What You'll Need

- lightweight cardboard, 8½" x 11"
- yarn, any color
- tempera paint or markers (various colors)
- two 12" wooden sticks
- scissors
- brass fasteners or rivets
- a hole punch
- heavy thread
- a pencil
- glue
- a ruler

Directions

1. Start by drawing a person on the cardboard. Make sure the arms and legs are wide enough. Use the paint or markers to draw a face and clothing.
2. Now cut the person out of the cardboard. To make hair, cut some short strands of yarn and glue them on top of the head.
3. Get ready to perform "surgery"! Cut off the feet, then cut again at the knees, then cut the legs off at the hips. Now cut off the hands, then cut at the elbows, then cut the arms off at the shoulders. All that's left should be the head and torso.
4. Next, punch holes in the arms and legs and use the brass fasteners to reattach each limb (A).
5. Now make the marionette's strings. Cut six 4" pieces of thread. Then cut six 9" pieces of thread. Tie the ends of the 4" pieces to the fasteners at the back of your marionette's wrists, elbows, and shoulders. Next, tie the longer pieces to the fasteners at the hips, knees, and feet.
6. One by one, tie the free ends to the wooden stick, spreading them out across the stick. The threads on the marionette's right side should be on the right half of the stick, and the threads on the puppet's left side should be on the left half. Rock the stick back and forth and watch your merry marionette dance (B)!

Ⓐ

USE THE FASTENERS TO REATTACH THE LIMBS.

Ⓑ

49 Lion-Hearted!

Instead of throwing out old washcloths, save them to make a little washcloth lion face!

What You'll Need

- 2 old washcloths
- fabric scraps, old socks, yarn, foam rubber, cotton balls
- fabric glue (available at craft stores)
- tape from an old audiocassette
- sewing machine (or needle and thread)
- buttons
- scissors
- felt

Directions

1. Start by making the lion's face on one of the washcloths. Sew on buttons for the lion's eyes. Cut pieces of felt for the ears, nose, whiskers, and mouth and glue them on.
2. To make the lion's mane, pull out the tape from an audio cassette. Cut the tape into 4"-long strips. Then lay down the second washcloth and glue the strips along the four sides of it so that they hang out over the sides (A). Overlap some of them to add thickness to the mane.
3. After the glue has dried, put any combination of fabric scraps, cut-up socks, yarn, pieces of foam rubber, and cotton balls on top of the second washcloth. A handful or two should be enough.
4. Now place the first washcloth over the second one to cover the stuffing. Sew the washcloths together along all four sides, using small, tight stitches (B).

One Step Further

Try making a girl's or boy's face by sewing two washcloths together on three sides and then stuffing it. Use cassette tape or colored yarn for hair. Add facial features using felt and buttons.

Ⓐ LET STRIPS HANG OUT OVER EDGE.

THEN SEW ALL SIDES SHUT.

Ⓑ

A Dandy Desk Set

If this "leather" desk set were real, it would probably cost $200, but you can make it for just pennies!

What You'll Need

- a small glass bottle
- an empty frozen juice can
- a 12" x 18" piece of cardboard
- two 12" x 18" pieces of construction paper, any color

- an empty baby food jar
- masking tape
- brown shoe polish
- newspaper

Directions

1. First, lay down sheets of newspaper to cover your work surface. Clean and dry the frozen juice can. Tear off small pieces of masking tape to cover the outside of the can completely.
2. Now rub shoe polish all over the tape until all the pieces are colored brown. Once the polish is dry, you've got a pencil holder!
3. Repeat steps 1 and 2, this time turning the baby food jar into a paper clip holder! Next, make the glass bottle into a flower vase or a letter-opener holder. Cover a cigar box with tape and polish and use it as a letter holder.
4. Now it's time to create a desk blotter. Take a sheet of construction paper and cut out four right triangles with 3" bases (A). These will be the four corners of the blotter.
5. Cover the triangles with short strips of masking tape, then rub shoe polish over them. Lay a triangle on each corner of the piece of cardboard so that the right angles line up.
6. Next, carefully glue only the right edges of the triangles down on the cardboard. The edges that face toward the middle of the blotter should not be glued down. Insert the second piece of construction paper into your blotter, tucking a corner under each triangle (B).

Ⓐ

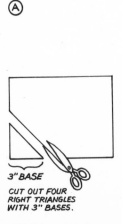

3" BASE

CUT OUT FOUR
RIGHT TRIANGLES
WITH 3" BASES.

Ⓑ

GLUE ONLY
THE TRIANGLES'
RIGHT EDGES.

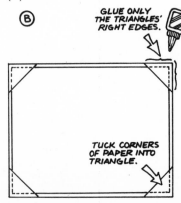

TUCK CORNERS
OF PAPER INTO
TRIANGLE.

Quick Freeze

You can magically turn water into ice without a freezer!

What You'll Need

- sponge
- paper cup
- glue
- scissors
- water
- pitcher
- ice cube

Getting Ready

Cut the sponge to fit snugly into the bottom of the cup. Secure it with a little glue. Right before you perform this trick, secretly place the ice cube at the bottom of the cup.

Show Time!

1. Pour a *little* water from the pitcher into the cup and say, "This ordinary water will now magically disappear."
2. Now ask a volunteer from the audience to kindly join you on the stage.
3. Slowly pour the ice cube from the cup into the volunteer's hand.
4. Say, "I really tried to make the water *disappear,* but it was just too *hard*!"

When you pour the water into the cup, the sponge soaks it all up!

SECRETLY PLACE ICE IN CUP

SECRETLY GLUE SPONGE TO BOTTOM

NOTE: The three cards in the upper right-hand corner indicate the level of difficulty of each magic trick, 1 being the easiest and 3 the hardest.

Big Squeeze

Squeeze a little glass of water so tightly that it vanishes into thin air!

What You'll Need

- a black elastic cord that is a little shorter than your arm
- a staple or pin
- safety pin

- a hard rubber ball that will fit tightly into the mouth of the glass
- small shot glass

Getting Ready

Attach one end of the cord to the ball with the staple or pin. Tie the other end of the cord to the safety pin. Fasten the safety pin with the cord tied to it to the inner lining of your magician's jacket at the top of the right shoulder (A). The cord and rubber ball should hang three inches *above* the bottom of your jacket. If the cord is too long, cut it from the top and retie it to the safety pin.

Show Time!

1. While standing in front of the audience, pretend you have an itch. The itch should be near your right hip. Reach into your jacket with your right hand and pretend to scratch. Take the hanging ball into your hand as you do this. As you withdraw your hand, make sure your knuckles are facing the audience and that the ball is well concealed in your palm with your last three fingers holding the ball in place. This technique is known as *palming*, and although it may feel funny, it is a very effective way to hide small objects. And, if you relax your other fingers, it makes you look like a great showman.

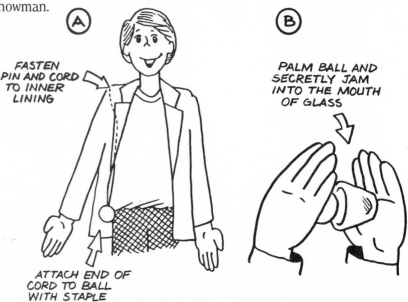

Ⓐ FASTEN PIN AND CORD TO INNER LINING

ATTACH END OF CORD TO BALL WITH STAPLE OR PIN

Ⓑ PALM BALL AND SECRETLY JAM INTO THE MOUTH OF GLASS

2. Pick up the glass with your left hand and point to it with your right hand (with ball still concealed). Say, "I've been practicing my powers of strength, and yesterday I squeezed a glass like this into thin air. Let's see if I can do it again."
3. Put your right hand on top of the glass and squeeze the glass between both hands with all your might. While you are squeezing, jam the secret ball into the mouth of the glass until it is tightly stuck (B), and straighten your arms out and down to stretch the elastic cord.
4. Turn slowly to your left and then suddenly throw your hands up into the air and yell "Shazam!" The glass will be pulled into your jacket so quickly that no one will see it disappear. Your hands will be empty!

NOTE: This trick requires lots of practice. When it is performed well, you will earn everyone's respect.

Classic Cups And Balls

Learn a classic cups-and-balls trick like the one magicians perform around the world, swiftly passing cups through balls and balls through cups. You'll be amazed to learn how easy this trick really is!

What You'll Need

- 3 cups
- 4 balls, either sponge or paper

(The cups must be stackable so that they "nest" together. They must also be tapered so the balls fit between the cups when they are stacked, without being noticed. The cups must be of a solid material so no one can see through them.)

Getting Ready

Place a ball into one of the cups. Stack, or nest, the three cups, *mouths up*, on a table. The cup containing the ball goes in the middle of the stack (A). Place the remaining three balls in the top cup.

Show Time!

1. Pick up the cups together in one stack and spill the three balls onto the table. This lets everyone see the balls.

(A) CUPS MUST BE STACKABLE AND TAPERED

HIDDEN BALL IN MIDDLE CUP

(B)

MOTION OF CUP

2. THE HARD PART: Everyone should see each empty cup but not the secret ball. Holding the stack of cups upright, take the top cup with your free hand and swoop the cup up and down through the air, then set it mouth down on the table (B). Repeat with the middle cup (the secret-ball cup). Place it over the upside-down cup on the table. (You should practice this several times beforehand so the ball doesn't roll out.) Place the third cup, in the same manner, upside down on the other two.

NOTE: Swooping your hand through the air actually helps force the ball to stay in the cup when it is upside down for a short time.

3. Tell the audience that you have no tricks up your sleeve. Pick up the cups in the stack, turning them right side up. One at a time, place them *mouths down* on the table, side by side. The cup with the secret ball in it will be in the middle. Remember to swoop each cup through the air before you put them on the table!
4. Pick up one of the three balls that you spilled out in Step 1 and place it on top of the middle cup. Cover it with the other cups, tap your wand on top and say, "Hocus Pocus!" Pick up the stack with one hand. Presto! The ball on the table must have gone right through the cup!

NOTE: This trick requires lots and lots of practice in order to achieve a flawless performance. The great thing about it is that once you've memorized the steps, you can perform it just about anywhere! Once you've become comfortable with the steps and can easily swoop and turn the cups over without spilling the balls, you can make up your own routine.

Five Glass Jive

Five glasses are lined up full, empty, full, empty, full. Ask a volunteer to change the order to three full glasses on the right, two empty glasses on the left—in one swift move, with one hand! Only you have the know-how to do it.

What You'll Need

- 5 glasses
- water

Getting Ready

Fill three of the five glasses with water. Line them up on a table in the following manner: full, empty, full, empty, full.

Show Time!

1. After several people try to change the order of the glasses, simply take the full glass on the right end and pour the water into the empty glass second from the left.

NOTE: Your friends will probably want to throw the water on *you* after this trick, so you'd better run!

Tip Over Tube

With your magic tube, change a white ball to red and back to white again!

For the Tip Over Tube:
- 2 small, empty vegetable cans (3¼ inches high, 2½ inches wide)
- colored adhesive tape
- black contact paper
- scissors

For the trick:
- the finished Tip Over Tube
- 2 rubber balls: one red, one white

Getting Ready

To make the Tip Over Tube, place cans bottom-to-bottom. Wrap tape around the middle so they stay together. Wrap black contact paper around the whole tube to completely cover the cans. Decorate the tube with colorful tape and glitter any way you like.

Show Time!

1. Stand the tube on one end and hide the red ball in the top part. Place the white ball next to the tube.
2. In front of the audience, pick up the tube slowly from the bottom. Quickly turn it over and put it down so the red ball does not fall out. Practice this several times. You'll be surprised how easy this is to do.
3. Drop the white ball into the top compartment of the tube. Your audience will expect the white ball to fall through, but when you pick up the tube, the ball underneath will be red!
4. To change the red ball back to white, turn the tube over again in the same, swift way, and drop the red ball into the top of the tube.
5. Lift the tube again and show that the red ball has turned back to white!

TWO CANS ARE TAPED TOGETHER BOTTOM-TO-BOTTOM

SECRETLY PLACE RED BALL IN THE TOP TUBE

What Water?

This marvelous trick is perfect for a real wiseguy. It is also very easy. The magician makes water disappear with a flick of a light switch.

What You'll Need

- drinking straw
- glass ¾ full of water
- colored or white adhesive tape

Getting Ready

Before performing this trick, practice drinking very quietly through the straw. Then hide the straw in your pocket.

Show Time!

1. Tape the glass of water to the table. Explain to your audience that you are going to make the water in the glass disappear without moving the glass or the tape. (Fastening the glass down is a little Houdini-like and will add some drama and suspense.)
2. Close your eyes and appear to be concentrating *very* hard. Pretend that you are trying to make the water go away with the power of your mind. Take a peek at your progress by opening one eye. When you see that nothing has happened, act really embarrassed. Ask for total darkness because you can't stand the embarrassment.
3. When your assistant turns out the lights, stomp up and down, bang your fists, and make a lot of noise. In the meantime, take out the straw. Use the noise as a distraction while you quickly and silently drink the water through the straw. Leave a little water at the bottom of the glass so you don't slurp and give the trick away. Quickly pop the straw back into your pocket.
4. Have your assistant flick the light back on while you stand there with a big grin on your face.

TAPE GLASS TO TABLE

The Tissue Tease

Craftily turn three pieces of wadded-up tissue paper into one piece of tissue paper with a secret message.

What You'll Need

- felt pen
- 1 large piece of tissue paper and 3 small pieces of tissue paper

Getting Ready

With the felt pen, write "Keep litter off the streets" in big letters on the large piece of tissue paper. Crumple it up into a ball and put it in your jacket pocket. Crumple up the other three pieces into balls. The audience will see these during the trick. (Instead of tissue paper you can use a heavy paper napkin. Unfold it completely. Cut off one-quarter for the big piece. Cut another quarter of it into three equal pieces to make the paper balls.)

Show Time!

1. Place the three little paper balls on the table in front of you.
2. Pick up two balls and put them in your left hand. Show the audience.
3. Pick up the third ball and put it in your pocket. Pull it out again as if you were changing your mind, but bring out the bigger tissue ball at the same time, hidden in the palm of your hand.
4. Place the third ball in your left hand with the other two. Immediately put your hands together and wad all the pieces of paper together with the big one.
5. With your left hand remove the *big piece only* from the wad now in your right hand. Make the audience think you've got nothing left in your hand by palming the three small balls and moving your fingers naturally.
6. Throw the big wad of paper into the audience as you casually place the small group into your pocket.
7. Ask the person in the audience who caught the wad to open it up. He or she will expect to find three balls. They'll be amazed to find *one* piece of paper with the very smart message!

SECRETLY EXCHANGE PAPER BALLS ⇨

SHOW OTHER TWO PAPER BALLS TO AUDIENCE ⬆

The Last Drop

By adding one more drop of water to a glass, make it impossible for a volunteer to lift the glass from a book.

What You'll Need

- hardcover book
- empty plastic tumbler
- pitcher of water
- large handkerchief
- eyedropper

Show Time!

1. Invite a volunteer onstage.
2. Hold the book in your right hand with your thumb on top of the book and your fingers below the book. Place the plastic tumbler on top of it. Pour the water from the pitcher into the tumbler until it is half full.
3. Cover the book and tumbler with the handkerchief.
4. Ask the volunteer to pick up the tumbler from the top through the handkerchief.
5. After the volunteer does this easily, ask him or her to set the tumbler down again. Remove the handkerchief and add one drop of water to the tumbler using the eyedropper.
6. Cover the book and the tumbler again with the handkerchief. Quickly shift your fingers under the handkerchief so that your thumb and pointer are above the book and holding tight to the bottom of the tumbler. The rest of your fingers are under the book. Steady the book with your other hand if you need to, but let the volunteer see that hand *above* the handkerchief. As you shift your fingers with a quick move explain that you forgot to say the magic words, "Hocus Pocus," that will make it impossible for him to pick up the tumbler this time.
7. Ask the volunteer to pick up the tumbler again. Because you are holding it by the bottom, he won't be able to move it at all!

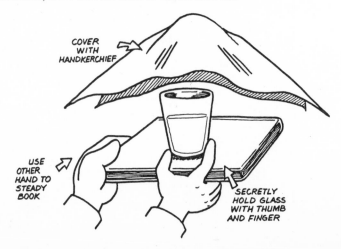

COVER WITH HANDKERCHIEF

USE OTHER HAND TO STEADY BOOK

SECRETLY HOLD GLASS WITH THUMB AND FINGER

Super Paper

Turn an ordinary sheet of newspaper comics into a bouncing ball.

What You'll Need

- hard rubber ball
- double-sided adhesive tape
- single sheet of newspaper comics

Getting Ready

Tape the ball to the top right-hand corner of the comics page in a criss-cross fashion (A).

Show Time!

1. Hold the paper in front of you by its upper corners with the ball facing you and cupped inside your right hand (B).
2. Say, "Believe it or not, I'm going to turn this funny page into a funny bouncing ball." Tightly crumple the paper around the rubber ball, and show the audience your great paper ball.
3. Chances are your audience won't be too impressed. That is, until you bounce it, and it comes right back up to your hand!

SECRETLY TAPE BALL TO TOP RIGHT HAND CORNER

CUP BALL INSIDE RIGHT HAND

Zap Ball

With ease and grace, you can make a rubber ball vanish into thin air!

What You'll Need

- 12 inches of black elastic cord
- small rubber ball
- tack
- pants with belt loops

Getting Ready

A useful part of any magician's tools is his or her clothing. In this trick, belt loops on pants serve as a quick spring-like device to make a rubber ball look as if it has vanished into thin air. To set up the trick, attach one end of the elastic cord to your middle belt loop (the one directly below your back). String the cord through all the loops on your left side except for any that might show when your magician's coat is not buttoned.

Next, attach the rubber ball to the other end of the cord with the tack. The elastic needs to be as long as the distance between the back belt loop and the first completely hidden belt loop. That first loop stops the ball from swinging away from you and keeps the ball within your reach, too.

Show Time!

1. As you complete the previous magic trick, take the rubber ball in your left hand and position yourself so your left side faces the audience. You want them to see the ball but not where it came from—pretend to have taken it out of your pants pocket. Because your left arm will be blocking the elastic from the audience's sight, the rubber ball will look perfectly normal.
2. With the rubber ball in front of you, the elastic will be stretched fairly tightly. Let go quickly, and no one will see the ball escape inside your jacket.

NOTE: This trick happens so quickly, it is more effective to perform it in silence. It does, however, require lots of practice to be pulled off effectively.

ATTACH ONE END OF ELASTIC TO BACK BELT LOOP; ATTACH OTHER END TO BALL

Ball Gone

With the flourish of a silk handkerchief, you can make a rubber ball disappear!

What You'll Need

- small rubber band
- multicolored silk handkerchief
- small rubber ball

Getting Ready

Find a handkerchief with as much design and color as you can. Secretly place the rubber band around the tips of your fingers on your left hand. Lay the handkerchief over your left hand, fingers pointing up (A). This won't be easy to do during a performance. You can either go off stage and come out again with the handkerchief draped across your hand, or, with practice, you can hide your hands below the tabletop so your audience can't see you put on the rubber band. Place the handkerchief over your hand as you stand up straight again.

Show Time!

1. Poke one of your right fingers down into the center of the rubber band to form a pocket in the handkerchief. The audience will not be able to see the rubber band.
2. Place the ball into the pocket (A) and close your left fist and your right fist around it and the handkerchief. Say, "This little ball will now disappear before your very eyes."
3. With your right hand, grasp one corner of the handkerchief and give it a quick shake, while letting go with your left hand. The ball will be gone!
4. After you grasp and shake the handkerchief, hold it down at your side so the audience will not notice the "secret compartment (B)."

THE SECRET: the tight rubber band will close around the ball, making a neat secret compartment!

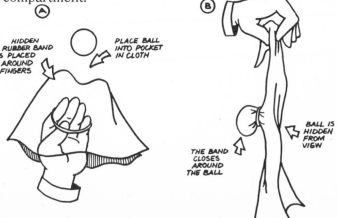

HIDDEN RUBBER BAND IS PLACED AROUND FINGERS

PLACE BALL INTO POCKET IN CLOTH

BALL IS HIDDEN FROM VIEW

THE BAND CLOSES AROUND THE BALL

The Ball Tube

A ball is dropped into a long tube. At your command, the ball stops and starts again until it finally drops through the other end.

What You'll Need

- cardboard mailing tube
- long sturdy needle
- black thread
- ball that fits snugly in the tube but rolls through easily

- small black bead
- black tempera paint
- paintbrush
- glitter
- glue
- ruler

Getting Ready

To make the tube, paint the mailing tube solid black and let it dry completely. Use the needle to poke a hole in the tube about seven inches from the end. Poke another hole directly across from the first hole. Thread the needle and push it into one hole and out the other hole. Tie a knot at the end of the thread to stop it from going all the way through.

Next, string the bead onto the thread. Tie the bead to the outside end of the thread so that when the bead is touching the tube, the thread inside the tube is loose (about twice the width of the tube) (A). When the bead is pulled away from the tube, the thread should be pulled tight across the inside of the tube.

Decorate the tube with different colors of glitter in any pattern you like.

Show Time!

1. Hold the tube straight up and down so that the bead is hidden under your thumb. With the bead in position next to the tube, drop the ball in the tube. It will fall right through.
2. Secretly pull the bead along the side of the tube with your thumb and drop the ball in the tube again. This time, the ball will seem to be magically suspended inside the tube (B). It won't fall out!
3. Secretly let go of the bead, and the ball will tumble out again!

Repeat this trick a few times for added effect.

(A)

THREAD RUNS THROUGH TUBE AND IS FIXED TO BEAD

(B)

BEAD IS SECRETLY PULLED; THREAD GOES TAUT AND STOPS BALL

Strawberry Milk

This is a famous trick performed by many magicians including the Amazing Randi. Here are the steps and directions to make it especially easy.

In this amazing trick, the audience will see you turn plain milk into strawberry milk with only a piece of fabric!

What You'll Need

- construction paper, any color
- clear adhesive tape
- piece of white cloth
- 2 glasses
- container of milk
- red food coloring
- piece of cloth with red strawberries on it (bought at fabric store)
- stirring wand
- eyedropper

Getting Ready

Roll up a sheet of construction paper to make a tube large enough to conceal one of the glasses. Fasten it with tape. Next, make a cone with another sheet of paper. The pointed end should fit inside the other glass. Before fastening the cone with tape, make a secret pocket with a square of construction paper of the same color. Tape three sides down, leaving the fourth open. Then roll up the cone with the pocket on the inside and fasten the cone together with the tape.

Next, fold the white cloth and slide it into the secret pocket in the cone.

To prepare the table, set the cone, one empty glass, and the piece of strawberry cloth on one side of the table. On the other side, set the tube, the container of milk, and the other glass. Put 3 to 4 drops of the red food coloring into this glass. No one will see them.

Show Time!

1. Place the pointed end of the cone into the empty glass on one side of the table.
2. Stand the tube on end on the other side of the table. Put the second glass into it.

WHITE CLOTH IS HIDDEN IN CONE

TUMBLER WITH A FEW DROPS OF RED FOOD COLORING INSIDE TUBE

3. Pour the milk from the container into the glass that is in the tube.
4. Hold the strawberry cloth up to the audience for inspection. Carefully fold it up as flat as possible and slide it into the secret pocket of the cone alongside the piece of white cloth. (Practice this before the performance until you can do it smoothly without looking like you are setting anything up.)
5. With the wand, pretend to stir the cloth around in the cone. Next, stir the milk in the glass inside the tube.
6. Tell the audience that the strawberries have been magically removed from the cloth and transferred to the milk.
7. Lift the *plain* cloth out of the cone and show it to the audience.
8. Lift the tube to reveal the glass of pink milk! "Boy, I love strawberry milk," you say. Take a sip! "Mmmm."

Ribbons Around Us

Pull yards and yards of ribbon from an empty hat!

What You'll Need

- 2 to 3 tightly wound colored paper ribbon rolls
- hat with an inner band

Getting Ready

Before the magic show begins, tuck all the rolls of ribbon under the band inside the hat.

Show Time!

1. Pick up the hat from the table. Put it on and spin it around, then take it off and show the audience both the inside and the outside. The band should hold the ribbons securely.
2. After everyone is convinced the hat is empty, set it forcefully upside down on the table. The ribbon rolls should drop into the bottom of the hat.
3. Reach into the hat and grab the ends of the rolls. Hold your other hand over the top of the hat and pull the ribbons up through your fingers from your supposedly empty hat!

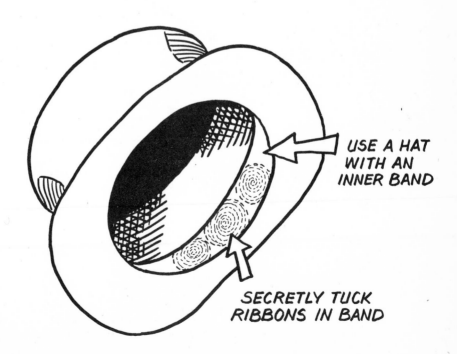

USE A HAT WITH AN INNER BAND

SECRETLY TUCK RIBBONS IN BAND

Breakthrough!

A volunteer magically escapes after being tied up!

What You'll Need

- 2 five-foot pieces of non-elastic cord or light-to-medium rope
- five-inch piece of thread
- 3 volunteers

Getting Ready

To make this trick work, both ropes are folded in half. The thread is used to tie a loop around the two folded ends. The loop is covered, and the illusion of two long, single ropes is created. In this trick, you need only a fist to cover the secret loop (A).

Show Time!

1. Have three volunteers stand side-by-side on stage, facing the audience. The two people on the end should stand forward, closer to the audience.
2. Holding the ropes with your fist clasped tightly around the secret loop in the middle, approach the volunteer in the middle.

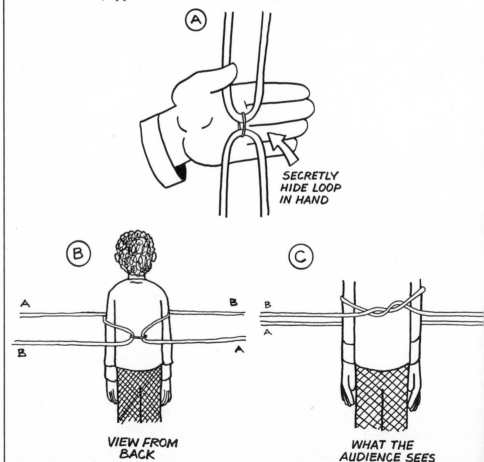

Ⓐ

SECRETLY HIDE LOOP IN HAND

Ⓑ

A

B

B

A

VIEW FROM BACK

Ⓒ

B

A

WHAT THE AUDIENCE SEES

3. Stand in front of that volunteer with your back to the audience. Bring the ropes over the volunteer's head and place them against his or her back. The secret loop should be in the center of the volunteer's back.
4. Ask the volunteer to hold the ropes loosely with both hands at each side.
5. Give the left ends of the ropes to the volunteer on the left and the right ends to the volunteer on the right. The result should look as though the outer volunteers are holding two long ropes and the middle volunteer is standing in front of the ropes (B).
6. Take one end from each of the outer volunteers.
7. Tie the ends loosely around the front of the middle volunteer's waist.
8. Step 7 will have switched the ends of the rope. Give each switched end to the outer volunteers. The middle one now appears to be bound by the ropes (C).
9. Ask the volunteers holding the ends of the ropes to pull hard on the count of three. The middle volunteer will be free from the ropes and the other two will be holding two ropes by the opposite ends!

Lions And Tigers

A member of the audience will see lions and tigers with the mention of just two magic words!

- paper
- pencil

1. Ask a volunteer to stand up in the audience.
2. Tell him that you know two magic words that will make him see lions and tigers. Ask him to close his eyes.
3. While the volunteer's eyes are closed, write the words "lions" and "tigers" on the piece of paper.
4. Tell him to open his eyes. Ask, "What do you see?"
5. The volunteer will have no choice but to say "lions and tigers!!"

Balloon Magic

Pop a balloon and watch it magically change colors!

What You'll Need

- light-colored balloon and dark-colored balloon (do not inflate them)
- straight pin

Getting Ready

Before your show, stuff the light-colored balloon into the dark one, making sure the mouths of the balloons stay together. Tuck the pin into the sleeve of your jacket.

Show Time!

1. Blow up the two balloons together.
2. Hold the mouth of the inner balloon closed and breathe a little more air into the outer balloon. Pinch both openings tight (A).
3. Hold the balloon up for the audience to see.
4. Casually remove the pin from your sleeve. Pass your hand over the balloon a few times. Pop the outer balloon (B). It will automatically "change" to a light color!

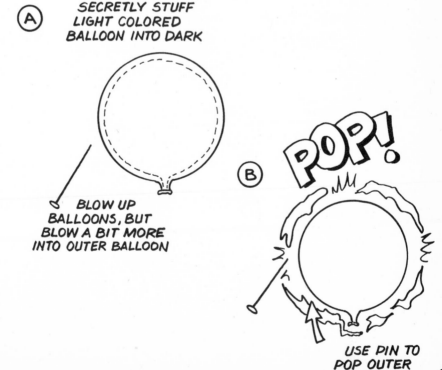

(A) SECRETLY STUFF LIGHT COLORED BALLOON INTO DARK

BLOW UP BALLOONS, BUT BLOW A BIT MORE INTO OUTER BALLOON

(B) POP!

USE PIN TO POP OUTER BALLOON

Flea Circus

You have trained your pet flea to perform for a live audience!

- blank sheet of paper
- small box with lid
- wooden pencil

Getting Ready

Preparing for this trick requires a little bit of practice. Hold the paper in your hand with the pencil underneath it. Practice pressing the paper hard against the pencil with your thumb. Slightly moving the paper forward with your thumb will create a small *pop*. Before you go onstage, put the little box in your pocket.

Show Time!

1. Tell a story about your remarkable flea named Fleaberta. The story can be told however you like, but these are the basic elements:
Fleaberta is an invisible flea who used to perform with gypsy fleas on pets in France. She traveled here on the back of a sailor's parrot. You found her in front of the flea market performing stunning acrobatic tricks.
2. "Fleaberta will now perform," you say. With your empty hand, reach into your pocket for the box.
3. Put the box on the table and open it. Say, "Fleaberta, would you join us, please?"
4. Pretend Fleaberta has jumped into your hand by following her with your eyes.
5. Hold Fleaberta out to your side in the palm of your hand. Hold the paper out at your other side to create a surface.
6. Toss Fleaberta into the air over your head. Follow her with your eyes until she reaches the paper. Pop the paper with the pencil when you think Fleaberta has had long enough to flip and land on the paper.
7. Ask Fleaberta to perform many stunts. Make them complex. Make them funny! It's all in how you move your eyes!
8. Make sure Fleaberta receives a nice round of applause.

Termite Damage

Another bugged trick! Discover termites in your pencil. Let everyone hear them!

What You'll Need

- wooden pencil
- paper

Show Time!

1. Take the pencil from your pocket and get ready to write on the paper.
2. Stop suddenly and hold the pencil to your ear as if you've heard something.
3. Exclaim, "Gee! I thought I had those termites exterminated!"
4. Everyone will look at you as if you're crazy, but try to convince them that there are termites in your pencil. "They *were* exterminated, but now they're back."
5. Pick a volunteer and hold the pencil up to his ear. With your hand next to his ear but away from his vision, scratch the pencil gently with your fingernail. The person *will* hear termites!

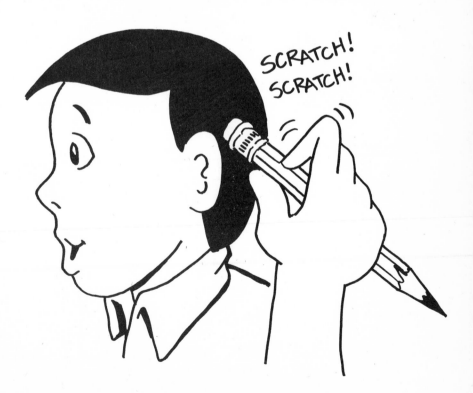

SCRATCH! SCRATCH!

Napkin Action

In this trick of wit and smarts, you can impress your audience with your strength as you pick up a whole bucket of rocks with just a paper napkin!

What You'll Need

- small bucket with handle
- enough small and medium-sized rocks to fill the bucket
- several paper napkins

Getting Ready

Test different napkins before performing this trick. Find one that is weak when open and strong when twisted up. Then, fill the bucket with rocks. Set it on the table just before you perform this trick. Unfold all the napkins and pile them up next to the bucket.

Show Time!

1. Ask your audience, "How many of these rocks in the bucket do you think you can lift 12 inches off the table with one napkin?"
2. Let a few volunteers try to do this. Most will put the rocks on a napkin and the napkin will definitely break.
3. Say, "I'll bet I can lift all the rocks in the pail with just one napkin!"
4. Lay an unfolded napkin on the table. Fold it over 3 or 4 times to make a thick strip.
5. Twist the strip. The napkin is suddenly much stronger!
6. Slide the napkin under the handle of the bucket, and lift.

Ice Slice

Cut a piece of ice in two, but see it remain in one single piece!

What You'll Need

- piece of thin, strong wire 9 to 12 inches long
- 2 pencils
- empty glass bottle, such as a soft drink or ketchup bottle
- ice cube kept in the freezer until you are ready to use it

Getting Ready

First you will need to make a tool to slice your ice cube. Take one pencil and wrap one end of the wire around the middle several times. Take the other pencil and do the same thing with the other end of the wire. The wire will cut through the ice and the pencils will serve as grips or handles.

Show Time!

1. Take the ice cube from the freezer and place it on top of the empty bottle.
2. Place the wire over the top of the ice cube so that it will slice through the middle of the cube.
3. Slowly, pull the wire down through the ice cube by firmly holding the pencil handles. It should take 3 to 7 minutes to cut through the ice. Have your assistant hold onto the bottom of the bottle to help steady it. In the meantime, you can tell a joke or you may want to build the suspense by being absolutely quiet. A drum roll is always effective!
4. Once the wire is close to cutting all the way through the ice, tell the audience that something incredible is about to happen. Keep cutting. The wire will touch the top of the glass bottle. Let the pencil handles drop and dangle from either side of the bottle. Pick up the ice cube. The audience will be amazed to see that the ice cube is still in one *uncut* piece!

NOTE: The trick is to allow enough time to let the ice *refreeze* after the wire has cut through it. Don't become impatient and cut too fast!

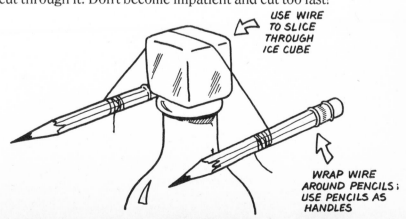

USE WIRE TO SLICE THROUGH ICE CUBE

WRAP WIRE AROUND PENCILS; USE PENCILS AS HANDLES

Spooky Shenanigans

In this trick, spooks seem to toss a wide array of objects over a shield made by a handkerchief that you hold with *both* hands.

What You'll Need

- straight pin
- large handkerchief
- ruler
- pencil
- small bell
- deck of cards
- set of keys

Getting Ready

Attach the pin to one corner of the handkerchief. Set all the items, except the handkerchief, on the table in front of you. Place the handkerchief in a bundle next to the pile of objects.

Show Time!

1. Show the various items on the table to the audience.
2. Pick up the handkerchief. Hold the corner with the pin in your right hand and the adjacent corner with your left hand. Keep the pin hidden in your fingertips (A).

HIDDEN PIN

SECRETLY USE PIN TO AFFIX HANKY TO SLEEVE

WITH HIDDEN FREE HAND, TOSS ITEMS FROM BEHIND CLOTH

3. Holding the handkerchief as described in Step 2, revolve your arms so your right hand moves in toward your left armpit and your left hand moves out toward your right shoulder (B).
4. Lower the handkerchief's bottom edge to the table so that it conceals all the objects behind it.
5. Secretly pull the pin from the corner of the handkerchief with your right hand (this takes practice!) and attach the pin and the corner of the handkerchief to your left sleeve close to your armpit.
6. Tell the audience something really spooky is going to happen ("Now, for the *really* spooky part!").
7. Your right hand is now free to move around because the corner of the handkerchief is secretly pinned to your jacket! Toss the items from behind the cloth, over the top, toward the audience (C). They'll howl with delight!
8. To end the trick, simply remove the pin from your sleeve and revolve your arms back to their original position. The spooks are gone!!

Magic Bottle

Watch a bottle dangle from a rope too thin to hold it!

What You'll Need

- glass bottle
- small rubber ball
- 1 to 2 feet of thin cord or rope
- opaque paint
- paintbrush

Getting Ready

Paint the bottle to make it totally opaque. Find a ball that, when placed side by side with the rope, will equal the diameter of the neck of the bottle. Slip the ball into the bottle before you perform this trick.

Show Time!

1. Hold the bottle in one hand in front of the audience.
2. At the same time, hold the rope in your other hand.
3. Lower the rope into the bottle, slowly turning the bottle upside down. The ball will fall into the neck of the bottle and wedge against the rope.
4. Pull the rope out toward you just slightly. This action will tighten the wedge inside.
5. Take the free end of the rope and hold it up. The bottle magically hangs from the rope without falling!

HIDDEN BALL WEDGES ROPE IN NECK OF BOTTLE

Finger Frustration

With the mere wave of a wand, freeze an unsuspecting volunteer's fingers together! This is a great beginner's magic trick and most people love to be included in it. It is a great crowd gatherer. Try this one on your friends at school!

Show Time!

1. Ask a friend to volunteer. "It's for an experiment!" you say.
2. Tell your friend to make fists and put them together, palms down, knuckle to knuckle.
3. Ask her to extend both ring fingers upward so their tips touch. The knuckles should still be touching. This is not an easy move for most. It may take awhile.
4. Wave your hands or magic wand over your friend's hands. Say, "You now have been drained of all power from your ring fingers." (You can laugh devilishly for added effect.)
5. What you see next is hilarious. Nothing happens! It is impossible to move the two fingers apart!

NOTE: This trick is even funnier if you have several volunteers at one time—try your whole classroom!

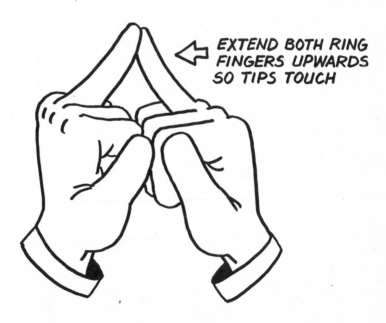

EXTEND BOTH RING FINGERS UPWARDS SO TIPS TOUCH

Mind Reader

Learn how to be a mind reader in this deceptive magic trick!

What You'll Need

- 5 to 6 different issues of the same magazine
- 5 to 6 copies of *one* issue of the *same* magazine
- paste
- scissors

Getting Ready

Before you perform this trick, find a magazine with page numbers. Cut off the front and back covers from all the different issues. Carefully paste the different covers onto the copies of the same issue. Place the "glued" magazines on the table in a pile when you are ready to perform the trick.

Show Time!

1. Invite a volunteer to pick up any of the magazines lying on the table.
2. Ask her to look at the last page number in that particular issue. Have her choose a number between one and the last page number and tell you that number.

PASTE DIFFERENT COVERS ON COPIES OF SAME ISSUE

USE MAGAZINES WITH PAGE NUMBERS

3. Pick up another magazine from the pile as if you are going to demonstrate to the volunteer what you want her to do. Make sure she sees only the cover of your magazine so she'll think it's indeed a different issue than the one she picked.
4. Ask her to turn to the page number she selected. Remind her what it is. Say, "Please concentrate very hard as you look at that page. Hold it to your head." Demonstrate how it should be done by opening the magazine to the page that was picked and glancing over it quickly, remembering photos and headlines.
5. As your volunteer holds the magazine to her head, pretend to be able to read her mind.
6. She'll be awfully surprised when you're able to give brief details of the page that she picked!

Some Enchanted Salt Shaker

Lift a salt shaker magically into the air without using your fingertips!

What You'll Need

- toothpick
- ring for your ring finger
- salt shaker

Getting Ready

Put the ring on. Hide the toothpick by tucking the end of it under the ring on the inside of your finger. Place the salt shaker on the table.

Show Time!

1. Slowly lower your hand, palm down, over the salt shaker on the table. Insert the secret toothpick firmly into one of the holes in the cap.
2. The back of your hand will be facing the audience to conceal the toothpick. Your fingertips should point down toward the table.
3. Pretend to levitate the salt shaker with your fingertips. The toothpick will stay in the shaker hole if it is jammed in tightly. This will mesmerize your audience!

SECRETLY INSERT TOOTHPICK INTO ONE OF THE HOLES IN THE CAP

My Thumb, Please!

In this beginner's magic trick, create a real shiver when you ask someone to hold something for you.

What You'll Need

- carrot
- handkerchief

Getting Ready

Find a carrot with a tip that is about the size of your thumb. Carefully cut a length of the carrot that matches the length of your thumb, and hide it in your fist.

Show Time!

1. Cover your fist with the handkerchief.
2. Poke the carrot up so it looks like your thumb under the handkerchief.
3. Ask someone to please hold your thumb through the handkerchief.
4. Once he has a good grasp of it, simply walk away with your thumb tucked into your palm. He's left holding what he thinks is your thumb!

HOLD
CARROT
IN HAND

Slip Knot

This amazing trick is easy but makes you look like a genius!

What You'll Need

- 1 silky handkerchief

Getting Ready

Before the magic show begins, tie a tight knot in one corner of the handkerchief.

Show Time!

1. Hold the handkerchief by its knotted corner, hiding the knot in your thumb and fingers.
2. Point to the lower end of the handkerchief, saying that you can shake the handkerchief so hard its free corner will knot back up on itself.
3. Bring the free corner up to your fingertips and the hidden corner. Shake the free end back down again.
4. Repeat Step 3 three or four times.
5. The last time you do this, shake the handkerchief extra hard, and release the knotted end instead. This move fools everyone. The audience will be astounded.

HIDE KNOT IN HAND

Not A Knot

This amazing little knot trick will keep your friends guessing for a long time!

What You'll Need

- magic wand
- handkerchief

Getting Ready

A magic wand can easily be made from the cardboard tube that is found on most hangers that come from the dry cleaner. Paint the tube black. Make white tips at both ends with white tape or construction paper. Glue thumbtacks to the ends to give your wand "tap-ability." Sprinkle on a little glitter or give it a nice shiny coat of varnish.

Show Time!

1. Ask a volunteer to help you undo a "double-twisting-sidewinding knot."
2. Have her hold one end of the wand and point the other at you while keeping it level.

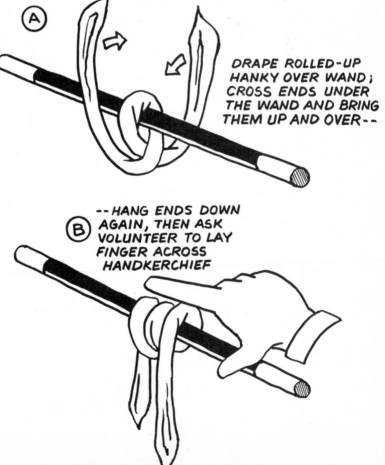

Ⓐ DRAPE ROLLED-UP HANKY OVER WAND; CROSS ENDS UNDER THE WAND AND BRING THEM UP AND OVER--

--HANG ENDS DOWN AGAIN, THEN ASK Ⓑ VOLUNTEER TO LAY FINGER ACROSS HANDKERCHIEF

3. Take the handkerchief by one corner and roll it up tightly.
4. Drape the rolled handkerchief over the wand so both ends hang evenly.
5. Cross the ends underneath the wand, and bring them up and over the wand, so the ends hang down again (A).
6. Ask your volunteer to please lay her finger along the wand over the handkerchief (B).
7. Repeat Step 5, but this time in the opposite direction. Bring the ends up and over your volunteer's finger, across, and down again (C), then up again so you can tie a knot over her finger (D).
8. Say, "By the time my helper moves her finger, this knot will have magically dissolved."
9. Hold the knot on top of the volunteer's finger and the loose end of your wand as well.
10. Ask her to pull her finger away quickly. Presto! No knot!

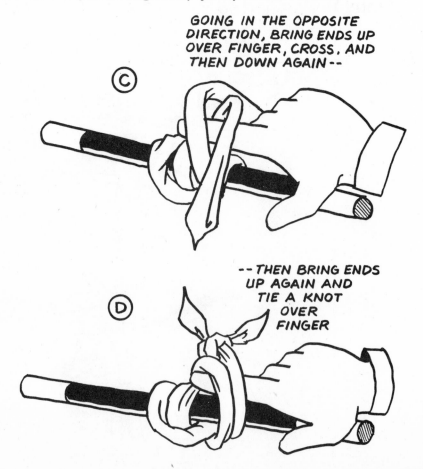

GOING IN THE OPPOSITE
DIRECTION, BRING ENDS UP
OVER FINGER, CROSS, AND
THEN DOWN AGAIN --

C

-- THEN BRING ENDS
UP AGAIN AND
TIE A KNOT
OVER
FINGER

D

Presto Hanky

In this complex trick, you will make a colorful handkerchief not only jump from one location to another but reappear tied *between* two other handkerchiefs!

What You'll Need

- 2 single sheets of newspaper
- glue
- whole newspaper
- 2 large red handkerchiefs

- 2 identical multicolored handkerchiefs or scarves with red borders
- empty goblet

Getting Ready

Make a secret envelope by gluing three sides of the single sheets of newspaper together. Leave a long side open (A). Place your newspaper "envelope" into the whole newspaper so it fits in normally, and keep it handy for the performance.

To prepare the handkerchief, follow these directions and look carefully at the illustrations.

First, take one corner of a red handkerchief and tie it to a corner of a multicolored handkerchief (B). Pick them up by the knot.

Next, lay the two handkerchiefs on a table, with the multicolored hanky on top.

Now, roll up the multicolored hanky lengthwise (C). Fold the roll back over itself so only the red border protrudes beyond the knot (D).

Finally, roll up the red handkerchief around the folded part (E). The final result should look like one red hanky rolled up. There should be no trace of the other one.

Roll up the remaining red hanky. It should look like the other one. Place both on the table.

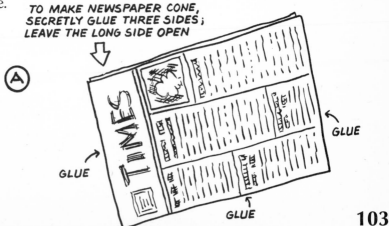

TO MAKE NEWSPAPER CONE, SECRETLY GLUE THREE SIDES; LEAVE THE LONG SIDE OPEN

(A)

GLUE

GLUE

GLUE

Show Time!

1. Hold the "magic" hanky in one hand with your thumb and forefinger around the knot. Hold the other red hanky in your other hand about one inch from the top corner. The two hankies should look exactly the same.
2. Tie the top corners of the hankies together. (The multicolored one should still be hidden inside.)
3. Wad the "two" hankies together, and stuff them into the empty goblet (F).
4. Next, you need to make a paper cone. Naturally, you reach into your handy newspaper and pull out the ordinary-looking single sheet of newspaper that you previously turned into a secret envelope.
5. Roll this sheet into a cone and hang onto it with one hand.
6. Take the remaining multicolored handkerchief, fold it in quarters neatly with your free hand, and pretend to slip it into the cone, but actually slip it into the big pocket you created.

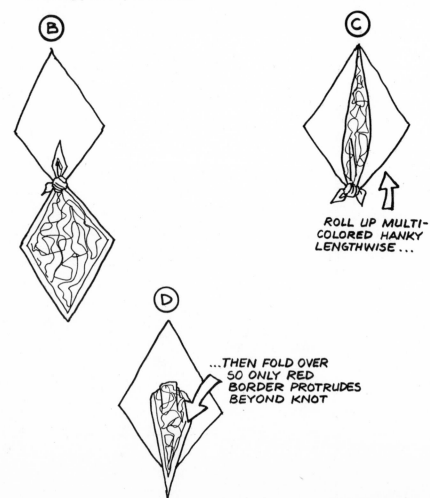

ROLL UP MULTI-
COLORED HANKY
LENGTHWISE ...

...THEN FOLD OVER
SO ONLY RED
BORDER PROTRUDES
BEYOND KNOT

7. Tell the audience that with the magic word "Shazam!" you will make the hanky in the cone join the red hankies in the goblet.
8. Reach into the goblet and quickly pull out one free corner of the hankies. The multicolored one will amazingly be tied between the red hankies!
9. Unroll the newspaper cone and show both sides of it. There will be no trace of the other multicolored handkerchief!

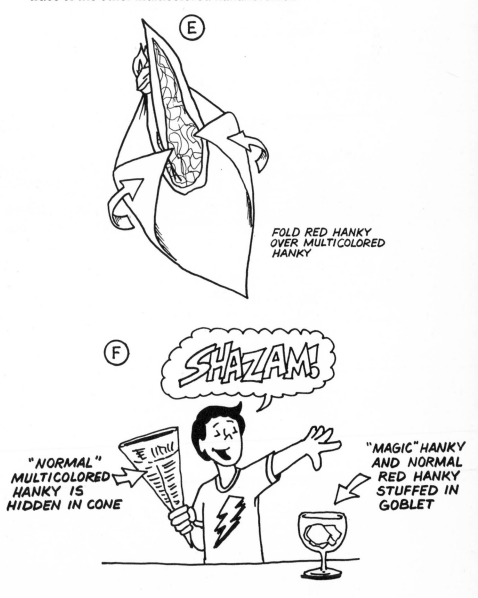

E

FOLD RED HANKY
OVER MULTICOLORED
HANKY

F

SHAZAM!

"NORMAL"
MULTICOLORED
HANKY IS
HIDDEN IN CONE

"MAGIC" HANKY
AND NORMAL
RED HANKY
STUFFED IN
GOBLET

The Ching-Chang Handkerchief Basket

With the mystical ching-chang basket, turn paper confetti into silk handkerchiefs!

What You'll Need

- large glass jar
- enough paper confetti to almost fill it
- black thread
- shallow basket
- 4 or 5 silky handkerchiefs

Getting Ready

Fill the glass jar ¾ full with brightly colored confetti. Tie one end of the thread to the edge of the basket. Cut the thread so that it is ¾ the diameter of the basket opening. Next, bundle up the 4 or 5 handkerchiefs and tie the other end of the thread around them. Before your performance, hide the bundle of handkerchiefs in the middle of the confetti in the jar. Set the basket right-side-up on top of the jar.

Show Time!

1. Pick up the basket in both hands and hold its open side toward the audience. The black thread will hang into the jar from the *bottom* edge of the basket. The audience will see just an empty basket with a jar of confetti underneath it (A).
2. Tip the basket forward, until its underside is facing the audience. As you do this, lower the basket so its edge just covers the top of the jar. The handkerchiefs will be pulled out of the jar and tipped into the basket without the audience seeing (B).
3. Continue to turn the basket in the same direction until it is right side up. Now hold the basket in the palm of one of your hands.
4. Reach into the jar with your free hand. Pull out some confetti and toss it in the air so it sprinkles down into the basket.
5. Pull out the handkerchiefs one by one from the supposedly empty basket! With practice this trick can be so beautifully and smoothly performed that even you will be astonished!

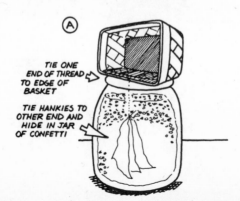

Ⓐ

TIE ONE
END OF THREAD
TO EDGE OF
BASKET

TIE HANKIES TO
OTHER END AND
HIDE IN JAR
OF CONFETTI

Ⓑ

TIP BASKET FORWARD;
HANKIES WILL BE PULLED
OUT OF JAR AND INTO BASKET

82 Out of Order

Roll up three hankies in a special order. Unroll them and they will be lined up differently!

What You'll Need

- 3 different colored handkerchiefs or cloth napkins

Show Time!

1. Place the hankies on a table, one on top of the other.
2. Roll them up together, starting with the hanky at the bottom of the stack (A).
3. Once two ends have flipped over as you roll them up, unroll the hankies (B). Their positions have magically changed (C)!
4. Roll them up again the same way, let *one* end flip over, and the positions will change again!

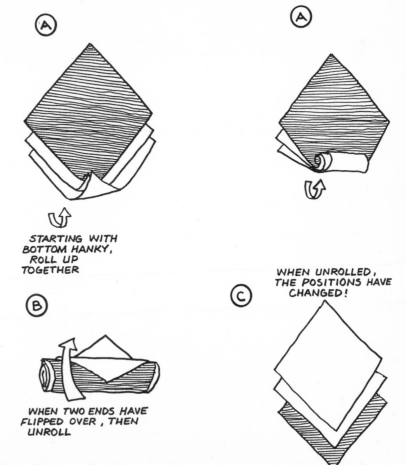

(A)

STARTING WITH
BOTTOM HANKY,
ROLL UP
TOGETHER

(A)

(B)

WHEN TWO ENDS HAVE
FLIPPED OVER, THEN
UNROLL

(C)

WHEN UNROLLED,
THE POSITIONS HAVE
CHANGED!

The Turning Box

The magical turning box is a source of great bewilderment to an unsuspecting audience. In this trick you will show your audience an empty box, both inside and out. Then, with a couple of turns, you will mysteriously pull out six handkerchiefs!

What You'll Need

- rectangular tissue box
- contact paper
- paper-towel tube
- adhesive tape
- scissors
- 6 large silky handkerchiefs

Getting Ready

To make the box, cut off the top of the tissue box. Cover it completely, both inside and out, with the contact paper (A). To assemble the device that makes this trick a success, cut the paper-towel tube down to 5¼ inches long. Cover it completely with the same contact paper. Carefully cut a square in the middle of the tube about 1 inch by 1½ inches. Seal the ends of the tube with adhesive tape. Cover the tape with contact paper and neatly trim the edges.

Next, tie the ends of the handkerchiefs together and put them into the tube one by one through the square opening (A). Put the tube inside the tissue box.

Show Time!

1. Hold the box between your hands, mouth up, and tube inside.
2. Gently set the box on the table.
3. Tilt the box toward you with your left hand without lifting the box from the table. The mouth of the box should begin to face you, while the bottom faces the audience.

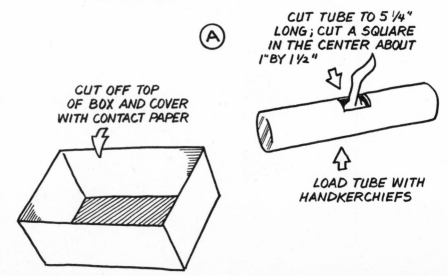

Ⓐ

CUT TUBE TO 5 ¼ "
LONG ; CUT A SQUARE
IN THE CENTER ABOUT
1 " BY 1 ½ "

CUT OFF TOP
OF BOX AND COVER
WITH CONTACT PAPER

LOAD TUBE WITH
HANDKERCHIEFS

4. Tip it a little more. The tube should roll out right in front of you. Block it with your left thumb so it doesn't roll too far. Meanwhile, tap the bottom of the box with your right hand to show that there is nothing hidden. This move draws the audience's attention away from your other hand.
5. Tip the box back to its original position. The tube is now *outside* the box, hidden behind it.
6. Tilt the box toward the audience to show its inside. The best way to do this is to slide the front bottom edge back toward yourself so you don't reveal the tube.
7. Keep turning the box in the same direction until the opening is facing you again.
8. Roll the tube back in the box with your left thumb.
9. Lift the box and place it in your right palm.
10. Reach in with your left hand, and use your fingers to hold the tube against the back side of the box.
11. Holding the box this way in your *left* hand now, reach in with your right hand and pull out the six handkerchiefs one at a time (B)!

(B)

SECRETLY HOLD TUBE IN HAND

The Disappearing Card

Here's a quick handkerchief trick to dazzle your friends!

What You'll Need

- toothpick
- handkerchief with a hem
- deck of cards
- scissors

Getting Ready

Cut the toothpick to make it the same length as the *width* of a playing card. Poke it into the hem of the handkerchief.

Show Time!

1. Spread out the deck of cards on the table.
2. Lay the handkerchief on top of the cards so that the edge with the toothpick in it is casually folded *underneath* the handkerchief.
3. Pick up the toothpick through the handkerchief with one hand. Hold one end between your thumb and forefinger. This will look as though you have picked up one of the cards!
4. Toss the handkerchief into the air and say, "Presto!" The card completely vanishes!

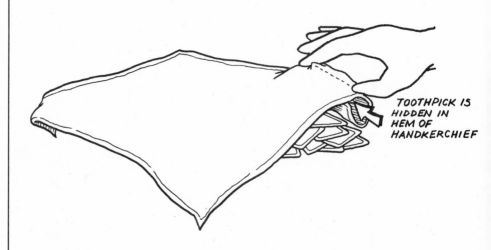

TOOTHPICK IS HIDDEN IN HEM OF HANDKERCHIEF

Good News!

Spread some fun and good news with this sneaky newspaper trick!

- empty sliding drawer box (matchbox style)
- rubber band
- 4 small silky handkerchiefs (red, yellow, green, blue)
- single sheet of newspaper
- scissors

Getting Ready

First, cut one end off the drawer part of the box. Slide the cover back into place. Stuff the 4 handkerchiefs into the box through its new opening. Now, place the rubber band around the width of the box. To prepare the newspaper for this trick, cut 4 slits in the sheet in different places. They should be just big enough for a handkerchief to be pulled through them.

Before you perform the trick, place the box under the newspaper on a table.

Show Time!

1. Begin by talking about the news. Using your left arm to gesture with and draw the audience's attention, slide your right hand under the newspaper, palm down, on top of the box.
2. While you continue talking about the news, slide the middle fingers of your right hand between the rubber band and the box. The opening of the box should point toward your fingertips (A).

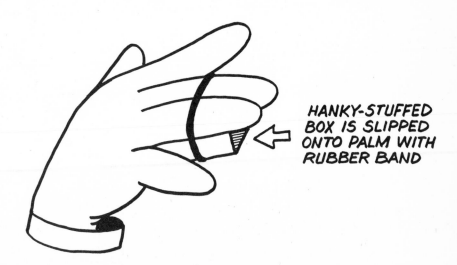

HANKY-STUFFED BOX IS SLIPPED ONTO PALM WITH RUBBER BAND

3. Sliding your right hand out from under the newspaper, grasp the paper between your thumb and fingers. If you hold the paper near the top in this manner out to your right side, no one will have seen the box attached to your palm or the rubber band (B).

4. With your left hand, point to different stories on the newspaper page. Trace your finger along the cuts in the paper as if you were reading. (Do indeed read from the paper but add your own last line to each story. You can use these endings or make up your own.)

5. As you get to your new ending of each story, reach into the cut on the paper and pull out a handkerchief! Remember in what order you put them in the box so you will know the order in which they will come out.

The endings: "So it turns out that everything ended up *rosy*!" (Pull out red handkerchief.)

"And they were *green* with envy!" (Pull out green handkerchief.)

"That car was a total *lemon*!" (Pull out the yellow handkerchief.)

"The Bobcats keep losing. They must really have the *blues*!" (Pull out the blue handkerchief.)

BOX IS
"PALMED"
AND HIDDEN
BEHIND
SLITTED PAPER

Break Out!

Just like Houdini, but on a smaller scale, remove an object from a maximum-security handkerchief! This trick even stuns volunteers from the audience.

What You'll Need

- man's large handkerchief
- large piece of black cloth
- key ring, 1 inch in diameter
- small object borrowed from the audience or supplied by you

Show Time!

1. Show the audience both sides of the open handkerchief.
2. Tell them you will trap an object in this handkerchief and then attempt to remove it by mystical means.
3. Lay the handkerchief on the table. Ask someone in the audience for a ring, a key, or a dime.
4. Place the object in the center of the open handkerchief. Draw together the far corners around it.
5. Put the key ring over the top of the corners, forming a little "prison" for the object.
6. Invite four members of the audience to help you "secure" the prison.
7. Each volunteer should take hold of one corner of the handkerchief and hold onto it tightly.
8. Drape the large black cloth over the handkerchief prison and the volunteers' hands.
9. The magic moment: simply reach under the black cloth and into the opening between the folds of the handkerchief to remove the object.
10. Show the object to the audience and the surprised volunteers. Gasps of delight will be heard!
11. Remove the black cloth from the handkerchief—the prison will be found totally intact!

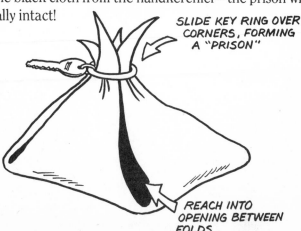

SLIDE KEY RING OVER CORNERS, FORMING A "PRISON"

REACH INTO OPENING BETWEEN FOLDS

Eggsibit

Put an egg in a hat and make it disappear!

What You'll Need

- needle
- thread
- handkerchief
- adhesive tape

- empty eggshell (you can find these at major shops, or maybe Mom or Dad knows how to "blow out" the contents of an egg)

Getting Ready

Using the needle, tie one end of the thread to the edge of the handkerchief, right in between two corners. Attach the other end of the thread to the egg with the tape. The egg should hang almost ⅔ of the way down the handkerchief (A).

Set the hat upside down on the table. Crumple up the handkerchief around the egg to hide it, and place it next to the hat.

Show Time!

1. Show the audience the empty hat, inside and out.
2. Lift the handkerchief by its corners so that the attached egg is on *your* side of the handkerchief.

Ⓐ

TIE ONE END OF THREAD TO HANKY; ATTACH OTHER END TO EGG WITH TAPE

3. Crumple up the handkerchief again and then draw the egg up from its folds (B). Show the audience that the egg has magically appeared!
4. Next, gently place the egg in the hat with the handkerchief around it.
5. Remove the handkerchief from the hat, again holding its upper corners with the egg facing you. No one will know the egg is there.
6. Repeat steps 3, 4, and 5 two more times.
7. Say, "I'm sure you think there were three eggs hidden in here," pointing to the hat.
8. Since you've been placing each egg that "magically" appeared into the hat, surely everyone thinks that's where they are. You now say, "Well they are . . . *not*!" Turn the hat over as you say this. Of course, there will be no eggs in it!
9. You can plan a surprise ending for this trick. Look all over for the eggs. Lift up the handkerchief to look under it, and "accidentally" (but really on purpose) show the audience the string and the egg. Say "Gotcha!" Your audience will appreciate being let in on *one* trick.

(B)

CRUMPLE UP
HANKY AND
DRAW EGG
FROM FOLDS

Tricky Pockets

You can create magic easily with several different day-to-day items including clothing! Here is a trick that utilizes your pants pockets.

What You'll Need

- a very large silky handkerchief
- a pair of your pants with front pockets

Getting Ready

All you have to do to get ready is examine your front pants pockets. Most pants have deep pockets, but they also have a rather large space of fabric in the upper corner that goes all the way to the zipper or buttons. What a super place to hide things! Wad or fold up the handkerchief and stuff it into this extra space before you perform this trick.

Show Time!

1. Say to the audience, "I have nothing in my hands. I have nothing in my pockets."
2. And then to prove it, turn your pockets inside out. (You can only pull out the deep part.)
3. Stuff your pockets back inside your pants.
4. Say, "I can pull a handkerchief from my pocket just by snapping my fingers."
5. Reach into your pockets again and pull out the hidden handkerchief.

NOTE: As you grasp the handkerchief, reach way down to the bottom of your pocket, so it looks as if the handkerchief came from the *bottom*, not the top, of your pocket.

HANKY IS PULLED FROM TOP OF POCKET

The Dancing Handkerchief

A handkerchief with a mind of its own? With magic, anything can happen! Learn how to make a knotted handkerchief dance itself undone in this impressive trick.

What You'll Need

- large silky handkerchief
- needle
- 2 to 3 feet of black thread or ultra-fine clear fishing line

Getting Ready

To prepare the handkerchief, secure the thread or line to one corner of the handkerchief with the needle. Tie a good, strong knot and lay the thread back across the handkerchief.

Show Time!

1. Gather up the handkerchief and tie a single knot in the middle of it, making sure the thread or line runs right through its center.
2. Hold the *un*threaded corner of the handkerchief in your fingertips. The threaded corner should be pointed toward the floor. The thread should hang down to the floor.
3. Step on the dangling thread. Point to the handkerchief and talk about its magical qualities while you step on the thread. Say, "This handkerchief is not just a dancer, it's a fancy dancer. It can untangle itself." This is called "drawing attention."
4. Next, gently move your hand up and down, back and forth to music as if the hanky were dancing and, right before everyone's eyes, the knot will come undone all by itself!

TIE A KNOT IN THE MIDDLE ⟹

MAKE SURE THREAD RUNS THROUGH KNOT AND DANGLES TO FLOOR

SECURE THREAD TO ONE CORNER

The Mystical Coin

You, the magician, can swiftly pass a mystical coin through an ordinary handkerchief!

What You'll Need

- large coin (no smaller than a quarter)
- handkerchief

Getting Ready

To get ready for this trick, you must practice. Only smooth, quick moves will give you the results you will need to astonish your audience.

Show Time!

1. Hold the coin up between your left thumb and forefinger in front of the audience.
2. Cover your left hand with the handkerchief (A).
3. Grasp the coin through the handkerchief with your right hand.
4. Fold the coin and the handkerchief toward yourself once.
5. Reach under the handkerchief, grasp the coin, and make a fold with your left hand (B).
6. Fold back the corner of the handkerchief, facing the audience, to show them the coin is still there (C).

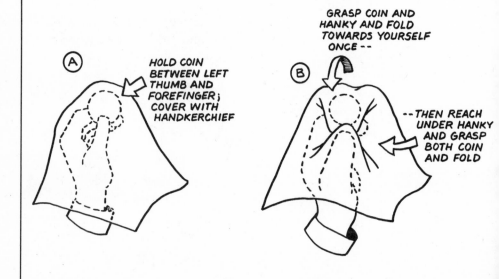

HOLD COIN BETWEEN LEFT THUMB AND FOREFINGER; COVER WITH HANDKERCHIEF

GRASP COIN AND HANKY AND FOLD TOWARDS YOURSELF ONCE --

-- THEN REACH UNDER HANKY AND GRASP BOTH COIN AND FOLD

7. What makes this trick work? Cover the exposed coin again—but instead of bringing back only the one flap of handkerchief, bring over the opposite flap as well (D). To the audience, it will look as if you just covered it up again normally.
8. Tightly twist the handkerchief just under the coin. It will appear to be wrapped snugly.
9. Work the coin out of the secret opening created by the folds of handkerchief (E). If done smoothly, even you will think the coin has risen up through the handkerchief!

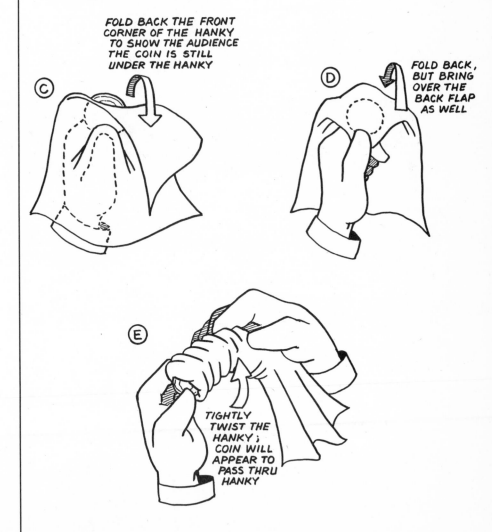

FOLD BACK THE FRONT CORNER OF THE HANKY TO SHOW THE AUDIENCE THE COIN IS STILL UNDER THE HANKY

©

FOLD BACK, BUT BRING OVER THE BACK FLAP AS WELL

D

E

TIGHTLY TWIST THE HANKY; COIN WILL APPEAR TO PASS THRU HANKY

The Sound of Silver

Half the fun of magic is knowing more than your friends do, or even pretending to know more, especially strange, unusual things like the difference between the sound of copper and silver!

What You'll Need

- 2 pennies
- 1 dime
- ¼-inch strand of your hair
- clear-drying glue
- sharp pencil
- 3 twist-on bottle caps

Getting Ready

Carefully glue the strand of hair to the penny so that the tiniest bit sticks out over the edge of it, just enough to stick out from under the edge of a bottle cap placed over the penny.

Just before your show, remember to put two pennies (one special, one ordinary) and 1 dime in one of your pockets.

Show Time!

1. Reach into your pocket and pull out the change. Take the special penny and the dime and put them on the table. Ask the audience if anyone can spare another dime.
2. As soon as you are given the dime, put the three bottle tops on the table. Invite three volunteers onstage.
3. Explain that your fine-tuned ears can detect the sound of silver. To prove it, you would like them to arrange the coins underneath the bottle tops any way they wish, one coin per top. Turn your back while they do it.
4. When you turn around again, ask the audience for complete silence. Tap each top with your pencil point.
5. Since the penny has the hair attached, you know which tops have dimes under them, making it much easier to detect the silver!

GLUE HAIR
TO PENNY

Colorized

The next trick is so much fun to do—and is so unbelievable—that you will probably practice it more than any of the others just to see the ever-amazing results.

What You'll Need

• deck of cards

Getting Ready

First, arrange the deck so that the top two cards are the same number or face but are in different color suits: one 4 of diamonds and one 4 of spades, for example. After that, you just need to practice to get the trick right.

Show Time!

1. Hold the deck face down in one hand.
2. Flip up the first card.
3. Slide that card, and the one right under it, about ¾ of an inch over the side of the deck (over the left side if the deck is in your right hand, over the right side of the deck if it is in your left hand). Be sure to slide them over at the same time so they look like one (A).
4. Hold the deck in your hand, overhanded. Throw the pack firmly but neatly so the stack remains intact, onto the floor. (Be sure not to do it *too* hard or you will be picking up a lot of cards!)
5. The rush of air will flip the top cards over, making the secret second card suddenly appear on top of the stack (B)!

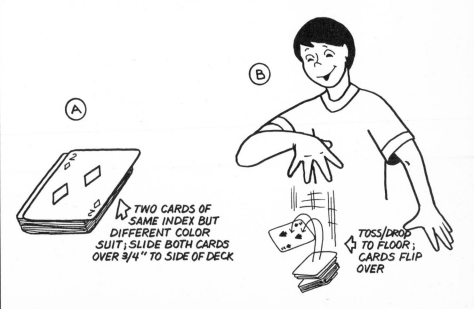

Ⓐ TWO CARDS OF SAME INDEX BUT DIFFERENT COLOR SUIT; SLIDE BOTH CARDS OVER 3/4" TO SIDE OF DECK

Ⓑ TOSS/DROP TO FLOOR; CARDS FLIP OVER

Penny-tration

Make a penny penetrate a human hand!

What You'll Need

- 7 pennies

Show Time!

1. Show your audience that you have seven pennies. Have a volunteer drop them one by one into your cupped hand and count them out loud.
2. Tell the volunteer that you can make one of the pennies pass through his hand.
3. Hold six of the pennies in your right hand and the seventh in your left. Making sure that the volunteer's hand is cupped, place the pennies into it one by one, counting them out loud. The first one won't make a noise, but the rest will clink.
4. Before you start putting the pennies in his hand, warn the volunteer that he must quickly close it once the seventh penny is dropped in.
5. When you get to the sixth penny, just clink it against the others in the volunteer's hand, and bring it out again hidden between your fingers. The seventh penny should be quickly dropped into your other hand.
6. Carefully and firmly cup your hand with the penny in it underneath the volunteer's fist so that his knuckles are facing downward.
7. Explain that it takes extreme concentration and incredible magic power to make pennies pass through skin and bones while you slowly flatten your hand against his knuckles. Now say, "Did you feel that? Look! I hold a penny in my hand. Quick! Count the pennies in your hand." Won't everyone be shocked to see only six pennies in the volunteer's hand!

PENNY IS
HIDDEN IN
YOUR PALM

A Head for Numbers

Use your mental powers to guess the name of a card right through a closed card box.

What You'll Need

- deck of cards
- the box in which it came
- scissors

Getting Ready

Before the start of the show, cut a very small hole in one lower corner of the box (A).

Show Time!

1. Spread the cards out on the table.
2. Hold the empty card box behind your back with its top open and facing away from you. The special hole will be facing upward. Hold it at its lower end, and cover the hole with your thumbs (B).
3. Invite anyone from the audience to pick a card from the deck, look at the card, and remember it. Then have the volunteer insert the card face up in the box and close the box while it is still in your hands behind your back.
4. The volunteer may be seated. Bring the box to your forehead. Say, "I can find out what card you had by reading your mind." As you lift the box over your eyes, glance into the hole to find out the identity of the card.
5. Place the closed box against your forehead with your eyes closed. Pretend to concentrate hard! You can even hum for effect.
6. Name the card. Your audience will be very impressed!

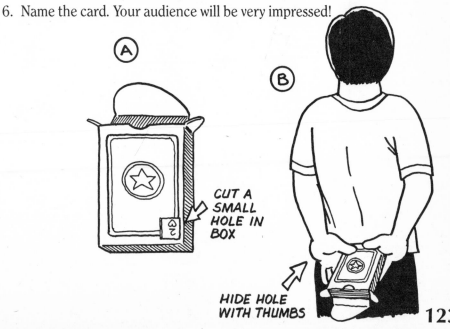

CUT A SMALL HOLE IN BOX

HIDE HOLE WITH THUMBS

Mental Telepathy

What You'll Need

- deck of cards

Getting Ready

Before you begin, pick out any two cards from the deck and put them in your pocket.

Show Time!

1. Ask a volunteer to choose three cards and show them to you and the audience. They can be from anywhere in the deck. Ask another member of the audience to concentrate hard on one of the three cards.
2. Put the three cards in your pocket with the other two secret cards. (REMEMBER! Note the order in which you place the three cards into your pocket.)
3. Draw out the two cards that you put in your pocket before the show. Don't show them to the audience. They will appear to be two of the three you placed in your pocket a moment ago.
4. Lay the two cards face down on top of the deck.
5. Say to the second volunteer, "If you have been thinking of your card, it will be the one still in my pocket." Ask her to name the card.
6. The volunteer gives the name of one of the three cards shown earlier. Since you carefully noted the cards and their order in your pocket, simply pull the audience member's chosen card from your pocket!

Houdini's Just Passing Through

Is it possible for a person to physically pass right through a playing card? With this funny trick, it is!

What You'll Need

- playing card
- sharp pair of scissors

Getting Ready

Preparation of the playing card is everything in this trick. Since you need to cut the card several times with a pair of scissors, you may want to practice a lot. You may also want a parent or someone good with scissors to help prepare the card for you. It is also a good idea to practice with ordinary paper, then practice on jokers or cards in an incomplete deck. Steps 2–5 can be done before the magic show.

Show Time!

1. Show the audience that you have an ordinary playing card. Tell them you are going to walk through this card.
2. Fold the card lengthwise, making a sharp crease with your fingernail or a pencil.
3. Starting at one end, cut from the fold almost to the edge of the card several times. Cuts should be ⅛ inch apart (A).
4. Now make cuts from the edge, almost to the fold, in between the cuts you just made (B).
5. Cut each fold along the crease except for the outer two (C). If everything is done correctly, you will have created one very long, delicate chain, big enough for a person to pass through.
6. Ask a volunteer to hold the long chain in an arch. When you walk through the special card, everyone will be surprised!

NOTE: Once you have mastered cutting the card, you can do it right on stage!

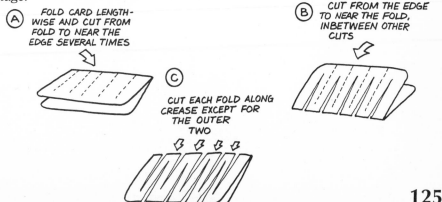

(A) FOLD CARD LENGTH-WISE AND CUT FROM FOLD TO NEAR THE EDGE SEVERAL TIMES

(B) CUT FROM THE EDGE TO NEAR THE FOLD, INBETWEEN OTHER CUTS

(C) CUT EACH FOLD ALONG CREASE EXCEPT FOR THE OUTER TWO

Discard

You can stump your friends over and over with this clever card trick.

What You'll Need

- deck of cards

Show Time!

1. Invite a member of the audience to the table to be your subject. Ask your volunteer to lay out two rows of cards, any number of them, as long as the bottom row has as many cards as the top row. You should be blindfolded or have your back to your subject. (You can even do this trick on the telephone with your subject!)
2. Instruct the volunteer to take one card away from the bottom row.
3. Now ask your volunteer to decide how many cards she would like to take from the top row. She should tell you this number and take away exactly that many cards from the top row only.
4. Now instruct her to take away from the bottom row the number of cards left in the top row.
5. Now tell the volunteer to get rid of the rest of the cards in the top row.
6. The object of having your back to the subject or being blindfolded or even on the phone is to correctly guess how many cards are left. The answer is always right if you remember the number of cards that your subject removed previously from the top row. It is always exactly *one* less than the number given!

Four Aces

Watch four aces magically jump from the pack to the table! This trick takes practice and careful, swift hand movements.

What You'll Need

- 2 decks of cards (both with the same back pattern)
- large pair of scissors
- ruler

Getting Ready

From one deck of cards, pull the ace of diamonds, ace of clubs, and ace of spades. Set the pack aside because it won't be needed anymore. Measure and cut 1/16 inch off from the bottom of each of the aces (A). Before the performance, take the three cut aces and the normal ace of hearts from the other deck of cards and set all four cards in a pile on the table. Place the remaining three normal aces seventh, eighth, and ninth from the top in the deck (B).

Show Time!

1. Tell the audience you have removed the aces from the deck. Point to the pile on the table.
2. Lay each ace face down on the table in this order: ace of clubs, ace of spades, ace of hearts, ace of diamonds. Let the audience see each one as you set it down.
3. Deal three cards from the top of the main deck on top of the ace of clubs, then the ace of spades, the ace of hearts, and finally the ace of diamonds.
4. Ask an audience member to call out 1, 2, 3, or 4. Count off each pile of cards so that no matter which number is picked, the pile with the ace of hearts is always the stack on which the count ends.
5. Put the other three piles back on the main deck. Shuffle the deck.
6. Snap the back of the deck with your finger and say "Ready." Slowly and carefully flip through the deck so the audience can see the top of each card. Surprisingly, there are no aces! (The cut aces won't be seen because they are shorter.)
7. Invite someone from the audience to turn over the stack of cards left on the table. What will be found? Four aces!

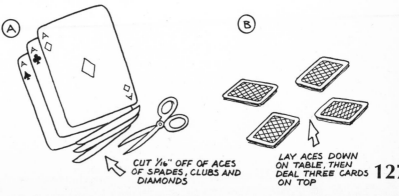

CUT 1/16" OFF OF ACES OF SPADES, CLUBS AND DIAMONDS

LAY ACES DOWN ON TABLE, THEN DEAL THREE CARDS ON TOP

All in the Voice

A volunteer's vocal vibrations will help identify a specific card in this mind-boggling magic trick!

What You'll Need

- deck of cards

Getting Ready

Before the magic show, place the four eights at the top of the pack and the four twos at the bottom of the pack.

Show Time!

1. Have a volunteer take the deck of cards in her hand and deal out all the cards into four piles.
2. After dealing the cards, ask the volunteer to pick one card from the middle of the pile, look at it, remember it, and put it on top of another pile.
3. Ask her to stack the four piles on top of each other. Then have her flip over and name each card, one at a time. Tell your volunteer that vibrations in her voice will give away the identity of the card.
4. As each card is named, listen for the number 8. If it is followed directly by a 2, you know that the chosen card is not near. However, when the number 8 is followed by another number or face card, and then a 2, the number in between the 8 and the 2 is the chosen card!
5. Ask your volunteer to go back and name the last few again. You can then announce, "That's it! I can feel the vibrations!"

PLACE FOUR EIGHTS AT THE TOP OF THE DECK

HAVE VOLUNTEER DEAL OUT ALL THE CARDS INTO FOUR PILES

PLACE FOUR TWOS AT THE BOTTOM

Fifteen Cents

Test your friends' math wit with this brain teaser at school or at a magic show!

What You'll Need

- 1 dime
- 1 nickel

Getting Ready

Before you begin, secretly place the dime and nickel in your hand. Make a fist around the coins.

Show Time!

1. "I am holding two American coins in my hand that add up to fifteen cents. One of them is not a dime," you say.
2. Pick a volunteer to figure out the problem. The answers given will be very surprising. You may not get any answers at all!
3. When you think the volunteer has had enough, open your hand and say, "I said one of them was not a dime, and I'm right—it's a nickel!"

NOTE: Get ready to run!

A Swing in Time

Think back to the last time you played on a swing. Do you remember rising higher with each push from a friend? If your friend pushed at the *wrong* time, you wouldn't get anywhere. Knowing why holds the key to many things.

What You'll Need

- seven pieces of string (one 24″ long, two 12″ long, two 8″ long, and two 5″ long)
- two chairs of same height
- ruler
- six large nails

Directions

1. Tie either end of the longest string to the backs of the two chairs as shown. Pull the chairs apart so the string is tight.
2. Using the ruler to measure, tie the remaining strings approximately 3″ apart on the suspended string, in the order shown.
3. Next tie a nail to the end of each string. You now have six pendulums.
4. Lift one nail (any one you like) toward you, then let go and let it swing. Push the nail at just the right moment so it swings even higher. What happens? Another nail will start to swing. Which one?
5. Try swinging a different nail. Which other nail starts to swing this time?

Why?

Every pendulum has a natural, or resonant, frequency at which it swings when pushed. (Frequency refers to how many times the pendulum goes back and forth per second. The longer pendulums have a slower frequency than the shorter ones). When a pendulum is pushed at its natural frequency, it will rise higher and higher—just as a swing will when pushed at the right moment.

In your experiment, when you swung one pendulum (say, the 8″ one), small vibrations of the same frequency traveled across the suspended string. When they reached the other 8″ pendulum, they pushed it at the pendulum's natural frequency, so it started swinging, too.

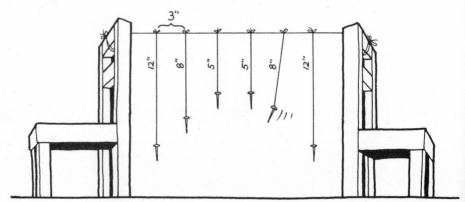

Let's Get into the Swing of Things

PARENTAL SUPERVISION RECOMMENDED

You may have heard that energy cannot be lost or gained. The swing of a pendulum demonstrates this well. In the next experiment, you can prove to yourself that energy cannot be gained.

What You'll Need

- an empty shampoo or other plastic bottle, with screw-on cap
- string
- a ceiling hook
- water
- a partner

Directions

1. Find a hook attached to a ceiling or ceiling beam. The area around the hook should be cleared of any objects.
2. Take a piece of string that's long enough to tie around the hook and still reach your chest. Ask an adult to tie the string in place.
3. To make your pendulum, first fill the shampoo bottle with water to give it weight. Have a partner hold the bottle while you tie the hanging end of the string around its neck.
4. Now we'll test conservation of energy . . . and your nerve! Hold the bottle and back up with it until you can hold it as high as your nose (but don't touch it to your nose).
5. Now let go and stand very still. What happens? Did you flinch?

Why?

When you lifted the pendulum to your nose, you had to do a little work. When you then let go, all the effort you used to lift it went right into the pendulum. In other words, the pendulum swung with the same amount of energy as it took to lift it up. On its return swing, the pendulum could only come as high as you had lifted it before, because that's when it ran out of energy. The amount of energy you give up is the amount of energy you get back. If, for example, someone had no money and you gave them a dollar, he or she could only give you a dollar back—that's conservation of energy.

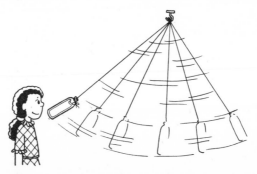

NOTE: The magnifying glass in the upper right-hand corner indicates the level of difficulty of each science experiment, from easy to hard.

Become a Film Star

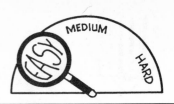

In this experiment you'll amaze your friends with your film talents.

What You'll Need
- medium-sized bowl
- finely ground pepper
- a gullible friend
- water
- a bar of soap

Directions

1. Before the experiment, secretly wet your index finger and rub it along a bar of soap.
2. Fill a bowl about three-quarters full of water.
3. Shake the pepper over the water for a few seconds. The pepper will form a film over the water.
4. Say that you heard some humans have an energy field around them that repels pepper—but only certain *special* humans. Have your friend stick a finger into the water. Nothing will happen.
5. Now stick your soaped-up index finger into the water. Wow! *Your* energy field works great!

Why?

Of course, it was the soap film on your finger that repelled the pepper. When you put your finger in the water, the soap quickly spread out in a thin (invisible) layer. As it expanded outward, it pushed away the pepper.

Yolking Around

Would you like to give a friend a raw egg to eat but make him or her think it's really hard-boiled? Do the following experiment and you'll learn how.

What You'll Need

- fresh egg
- hard-boiled egg, cooled
- a gullible friend

Directions

1. Have someone mix up the fresh and hard-boiled eggs so you don't know which is which.
2. Now take one egg and spin it. Take note of how fast it spins. Spin it again, then stop the spin by putting your index finger on the egg for a second. What happens to the egg when you take your finger off?
3. Spin the second egg. Does it spin faster or slower than the first egg? Spin the egg again, then tap it with your finger to stop it. What happens to this egg when you take your finger off? Why does one egg keep spinning? Can you now tell which is the egg you can hand over to your friend and be certain there'll be a mess for him or her to clean?

Why?

When you're driving down the road in a car and suddenly come to a stop, did you ever notice how your body keeps going forward after the car stops? (This is the main reason for seatbelts, of course.) When something is moving, it will continue to move until something stops it. If two things are rigidly connected to each other, stopping one will stop the other.

In a fresh egg, you can think of the shell as the car and the yolk as your body. When the spinning egg comes to a halt, the yolk is free to keep spinning because it is not rigidly connected to the shell. With the hard-boiled egg, however, you can think of the entire egg as the car, because it's solid through and through. When you tap your finger on the egg to stop it, the yolk stops when the shell stops—it has a seatbelt on!

Gravity as a Pump

Have you ever thought about what you would do in a flood? How could you pump the water out of your house without a pump? We'll show you how to use the earth's gravitational pull to do exactly that.

What You'll Need

- approximately ten feet of transparent rubber tubing, ½″ to ¾″ in diameter
- kitchen sink
- large-sized pail
- food coloring (any color)
- ladder (or stack of books)
- chair

Directions

1. Coil the rubber hose and put it in your kitchen sink.
2. Plug up the drain, then start filling the sink with water. Add some food coloring so you can better watch the flow of water later.
3. As you fill the sink, hold up one end of the hose to the faucet to get all the air bubbles out of the hose as you fully immerse it.
4. Plug up both ends of the rubber hose with your thumbs and bring one of the ends into a pail on the floor (A). Make sure the end in the sink remains submerged.
5. When you've got your pump in place in the pail, take your thumbs off and watch what happens. Why does the water drain out of the sink?
6. Let the water drain completely into the pail (but not out of the hose). Now perform the experiment again, this time draining the water from the pail back into the sink. To demonstrate that gravity is at work, this time place the pail on a chair next to your sink. Will the water drain?
7. Now lift the pail higher by means of a ladder (or a stack of books placed on the counter under the pail). How high does the pail need to be before the water in it will drain into the sink?

Ⓐ

Just as your body wants to come back down after you jump up, the water in the sink wants to come down (since it is above ground level). But it can't, since the sink contains it. With the hose to drain it, the water now has a way of getting down. The bubbles in the hose push back against the water, preventing it from flowing freely. That's why you have to get all the bubbles out.

The distance from the sink to the pail needs to be greater than the distance from the sink to the top of the hose (B). If not, the water will not flow. Can you guess why? (The energy needed to pull the water up to the top of the hose would be greater than the amount of gravitational energy available.)

Also, the higher the pail of water, the faster the flow. As you lift the pail higher and higher, you give it more and more energy. The water also has a greater distance to fall and thus more time to gain speed. If you put the pail on top of a ladder outside and let the water drain to the ground, you'll see how quickly the pail is emptied of its water.

- You may think that gravity is a strong force, but compared to other forces (such as magnetic), it is very weak indeed. Consider this: when you jump into the air, for a split second you actually overcome the gravitational pull of the huge planet you're standing on!

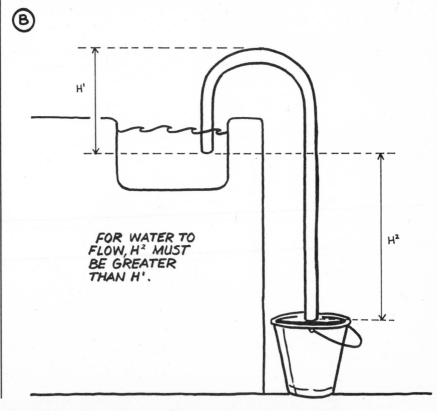

Ⓑ

H'

FOR WATER TO FLOW, H² MUST BE GREATER THAN H'.

H²

The Skater's Finale

PARENTAL SUPERVISION RECOMMENDED
As a last dazzling move, a figure skater will sometimes whirl in a tornadolike finish, spinning around faster than it seems possible—even on ice. How do skaters do it? Athletic skill has much to do with it, of course, but without a certain principle of science, the move couldn't be done. We'll let you observe this "hyper-spin" at work, then have you perform "the skater's finale."

What You'll Need

- two thread spools (without thread, or cover the thread with masking tape)
- approximately 30 inches of string (rawhide or a shoelace will do)
- pair of socks

Directions

1. Tie a knot in one end of the string, then pull it through the first spool so it rests on top of the knotted end.
2. Now pull the string through the second spool, leaving about four inches of string free at the unknotted end (A).
3. Find an open area to perform the experiment. Holding spool 2 with your left hand and the free end of the string with your right hand, swing spool 1 around as shown. When you've got it spinning fairly rapidly, note how fast it is spinning around.
4. Now stop spinning spool 1 and gently pull the string with your right hand (B). What happens to it? Can you explain why the spool spins faster?

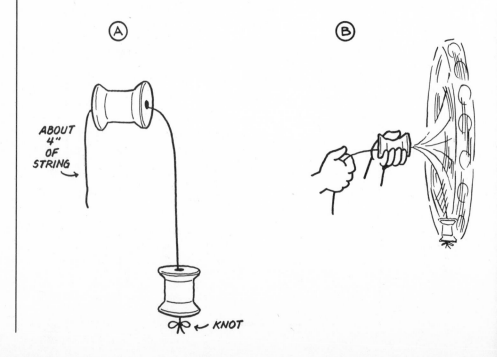

Ⓐ

ABOUT 4" OF STRING →

← KNOT

Ⓑ

5. Now you're ready for your performance on "ice." Stand on a linoleum or wooden floor with your socks on and your arms spread out. Spin around on one foot like a skater doing a pirouette.
6. Keep your arms outstretched for a moment, then bring your arms in close to your body as you spin. Did you notice that you spun faster when you brought your arms in?
7. Now repeat the performance, this time holding a heavy book in each outstretched hand before you start spinning. When you bring your arms in close this time, you'll notice that the whipping sensation is more intense.

Why?

In the first part of your experiment, why did spool 1 speed up? Well, since the spool was moving, it had a certain amount of energy. Then, when you pulled the string through spool 2, you did some work. This took energy, which you gave to spool 1. (Just as lifting the pendulum "handed over" energy to the pendulum, here, too, pulling the string handed over energy to the spool.) With more energy, the spool could speed up (C).

This same explanation can be used for your skating finale. Since you were spinning on the linoleum floor, you already had energy. Pulling your arms in took a little work. The energy from that work was transferred directly to your spin. So, you spun even faster. When you held the books in your hands, the effect became even more dramatic.

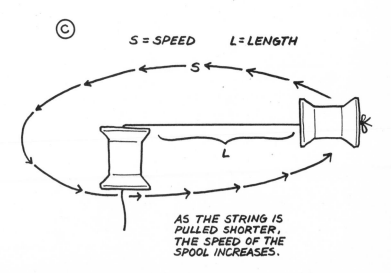

Ⓒ S = SPEED   L = LENGTH

AS THE STRING IS PULLED SHORTER, THE SPEED OF THE SPOOL INCREASES.

Instant Hercules I

EASY MEDIUM HARD

You've heard of the ancient Roman hero and strongman, Hercules? After you've performed this experiment, you can join his ranks.

What You'll Need

- a fairly large, fresh potato
- paper straw

Directions

1. Holding the potato in one hand and the straw in the other, try to ram the straw through the potato. Tough to do, right?
2. Repeat the procedure, this time holding your thumb over one end of the straw and ramming with the other end. Wow! How did you get to be so strong?

Why?

When the end of the straw was uncovered and you rammed it into the potato, it was very easy for the straw's flimsy sides to collapse. But when you covered the straw with your thumb, you trapped air inside the straw, and that changed everything. As the straw entered the potato, the trapped air became compressed and pushed outward (like the way a compressed spring pushes outward) against the sides of the straw. The air prevented the straw from collapsing, and you could push it through the potato.

Instant Hercules II

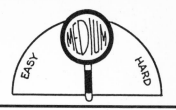

PARENTAL SUPERVISION RECOMMENDED

When you understand a few simple ideas, you can perform physical feats that would otherwise be impossible. For example, using a lever, you can move a boulder much too heavy to lift by yourself. This experiment involves the lever—a machine that demonstrates the principle of "mechanical advantage."

What You'll Need

- medium-sized pail
- two 2″ nails
- water
- broom with long handle
- tall chair or bench
- hammer
- ruler

Directions

1. Fill the pail with water and find a spot outside. With one hand, try lifting the pail as high as your shoulder. Can you do it?
2. Now we'll use some mechanical advantage. Hammer the nails into the broom handle (not all the way), one about three inches from the end, the other about four inches. Then place the broom over the back of a chair and place the pail handle between the nails as shown.
3. Push on the opposite end of the broom and lift the pail. Was it easier to lift using the lever? How high can you lift the water?

Why?

Lifting the pail of water off the ground takes the same amount of energy no matter how the job is done, whether by hand or by lever. In your experiment, it was easier for you to lift the pail with the lever because it gave you mechanical advantage. However, using the lever did not mean that you *did less work*. It just meant that you used the same amount of energy in a different, easier way—namely, it took you *longer* to complete the job. Using a lever is a lot like taking a long, easy trail to the top of a hill rather than taking a short, steep trail. The shorter way seems like it takes more energy (because it's steep), but it doesn't. Even though each step on the easy trail takes little effort, there are many more steps to take. Whichever way you choose to get to the top (or lift the pail), the total amount of energy used is the same.

Give Me a Lift

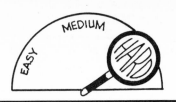

What You'll Need

Directions

PARENTAL SUPERVISION RECOMMENDED

If an airplane can weigh as much as 500,000 pounds, how does it manage to stay in flight? The reason has much to do with the principle of lift. In the next experiment, we'll demonstrate how airflow can create lift.

- an 8" x 11" piece of heavy construction paper
- scissors
- protractor (or jar 4" to 5" in diameter)
- tape
- plastic straw
- ruler
- hole puncher (optional)

1. Using the protractor (or jar), construction paper, and scissors, cut out a circle with a 4" or 5" diameter.
2. Cut out another piece of paper, this time a square with 5" sides. Set the square aside.
3. In the center of the circle, punch out a hole that's big enough for the straw to fit through. (If you don't have a hole puncher, use a pair of scissors to poke a hole through the paper, then twist the scissors around to increase the size of the hole.)
4. Put one end of the straw in the hole and carefully tape it in place as shown. (A). This is your blower.
5. Place the square piece of construction paper on a table and hold your blower about two inches above it. Now blow through the straw. As you might have expected, the paper was blown out of place.
6. Repeat the procedure, this time holding your blower about a half inch away. Blow hard on the straw and watch what happens. The square not only didn't get blown out of place, it got sucked up!

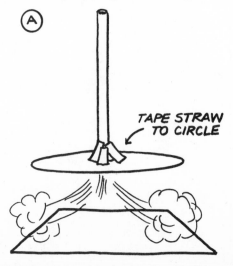

Ⓐ

TAPE STRAW
TO CIRCLE

Why?

There is a principle in physics that describes how pressure relates to the flow of fluids (air is considered a fluid). The principle says that as a fluid in a stream moves faster, the pressure on its sides decreases. You can test this for yourself by turning on your garden hose and pinching in the sides. If the water is streaming out very fast, it will be easy to pinch in the sides of the hose. But if the water is streaming out slowly, it will be much harder to pinch the hose closed.

The same is true of air. You created a stream of moving air when you blew through the straw. When you held the square piece of paper two inches away from your blower, the air couldn't be directed into streams (A). However, when you held your blower much closer to the square, the air was pushed outward between the blower disk and the square, forming two streams of rapidly moving air (B). The fast-moving (low-pressure) airstreams between your blower and the square paper pushed down less than the slow (high-pressure) air beneath the square pushed up (believe it or not, there is a layer of air beneath the square). So, the high-pressure air from below pushed the square up—lift!

Wonder List

• Why do lightweight objects get sucked out of a car window at high speed?

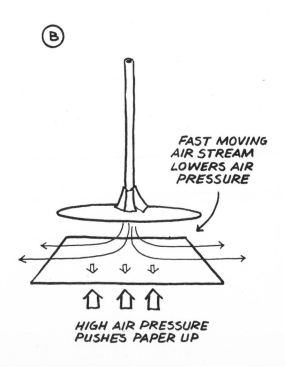

Ⓑ

FAST MOVING
AIR STREAM
LOWERS AIR
PRESSURE

HIGH AIR PRESSURE
PUSHES PAPER UP

Winging It

In this experiment, we'll build a wing and see how its curvature creates the kind of airflow necessary for flight.

What You'll Need

- pencil
- ruler
- strip of paper, as wide as the ruler and 4″ long
- tape

Directions

1. Tape one edge of the strip to the ruler so that it lines up with the 1½″ mark. Tape the other edge down at the ruler's 5″ mark. The paper "wing" should have a bulge in it.
2. Balance the ruler across the pencil. Then push the ruler a little past the balance point, so the paper-wing end seesaws down and touches the table.
3. Now, lay your chin down at the opposite end of the ruler and blow toward the wing. The paper-wing end of the ruler lifts up. How did that happen?

Why?

The curve makes the top of the wing longer than the bottom of the wing. Therefore, the air on top has to flow faster than the air on the bottom (under the ruler) to arrive at the back of the wing at the same time. The fast air flowing over the top pushes down less than the air below pushes up—so up it goes!

The Un-Waterfall

If held upside down, water in a pail will naturally pour out. Not always, though. Sometimes it's possible to defy gravity.

What You'll Need

- pail (or small bucket)
- water

Directions

1. Fill the pail about half full with water.
2. Now find an open area outside where you can perform the experiment. Start by swinging the pail at your side to build up momentum.
3. Then swing the pail around in circles, fast, like a baseball pitcher "winding up." Though swung upside down, the water won't spill out.

Why?

When you swung the pail up, the water started moving upward. Before it could reach its highest point, however, the pail got in the way, so you felt the water crashing upward into the bottom of the pail. This crashing accounts for the upward pull you felt on your arm. On the way down, the pail was moving faster downward than the water could naturally fall. So, the pail actually pushed the water from behind, and the water appeared to be stuck to the pail. Because the pail was always in front of (catching) the water moving upward, then pushing the water from behind, it seemed as if some mysterious force was holding the water in the pail.

Wonder List

- How can people successfully live in the zero gravity of outer space? One way is to simulate gravity. In the movie *2001: A Space Odyssey,* there was a giant spinning space station that looked like a wheel. Just as the water stayed pressed against the bottom of the pail, so, too, did the astronauts stay pressed against the floor of the space station—as if there was gravity.

Tire in a Gyre

PARENTAL SUPERVISION RECOMMENDED
Have you ever wondered how your bike stays up when you ride it? Why don't you just fall over? Believe it or not, your bike has something in common with our planet.

What You'll Need

- bicycle tire
- ceiling hook
- a partner
- string

Directions

1. Have a parent help you remove a wheel from your bicycle.
2. Hold the bolts on either side of the center of the tire (the axis) and have someone spin it as hard as they can (A). You've just made a gyroscope.
3. Now try to move your hands up, down, right, and left while holding the gyroscope. What happens? Feels pretty weird, doesn't it!
4. Next, attach the wheel at one bolt to the same string and ceiling hook you used in the Swing of Things pendulum experiment.
5. Hold the wheel parallel to the ground and spin it hard. Holding the two bolts, lift it (with arm movement this time, not hand movement) to a different angle and let go (B). What happens? The gyroscope will maintain its position no matter how you angle it, even vertically.

Why?

The strange forces you felt in trying to move the spinning wheel have to do with an interesting property of gyroscopes. When you push on something, it usually moves in the direction you pushed it. For instance, if you grab the ends of the bike-wheel axis and push forward (while it is not turning), the wheel will move forward. However, when you push on the axis of a *spinning* wheel (a gyroscope), it does not move in the direction you push it. Instead, it moves to the side. That's because the spinning redirects the force pushed against the wheel.

You Can't Blow It

It's easy enough to blow up a balloon. But what if the balloon is submerged under water? If deep enough, you'll find you just can't blow it.

What You'll Need

- two plastic straws
- bathtub filled with water
- a twist tie (like the ones used on plastic bags)
- balloon
- masking tape

Directions

1. Fit one end of a plastic straw into another to double the length of the straw. Seal the joint with masking tape.
2. Now insert one end of your double-straw into a deflated balloon. Push it all the way in until it is *almost* touching the opposite end of the balloon.
3. Wrap the twist tie around the lip of the balloon and tighten it (so that no air can escape the balloon when you blow it up).
4. Hold the double-straw and blow up your balloon. Notice how hard you had to blow to inflate it. It should be fairly easy.
5. Put the balloon under water as shown and try to blow it up again. Was it easier or harder to blow up the balloon while it was submerged?

Why?

You may not notice it, but there is air pressure pushing against you at all times. That pressure is the weight of the entire earth's atmosphere pressing down on you. Although our atmosphere is a whopping 300 miles high, it doesn't crush you because air is so light. Water, however, is much heavier than air—so much heavier, in fact, that only 33 feet of it is as heavy as 300 miles of air. This explains the problem in blowing up the submerged balloon. To blow up a balloon in air, the sides of the balloon must push out against the air pressure pushing in. This is easy for your lungs to do. But under water, the pressure increases dramatically. It's very difficult to push the sides of the balloon out against the water pressure pushing in.

Wonder List

- When diving, why do you need scuba equipment? Why not just use a long snorkel?

Boiling
at Low Pressure

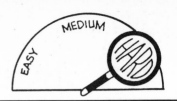

PARENTAL SUPERVISION REQUIRED

We usually think that a liquid boils because it's very hot. Usually, that's true. But not always . . .

What You'll Need

- 500-ml Erlenmeyer flask from a chemist's shop or toy store (with rubber stopper)
- 4 gallons of water chilled overnight in the refrigerator
- stove burner
- potholder glove
- kitchen sink with stopper
- tap water

Directions

1. Fill the Erlenmeyer flask to the 200-ml mark with tap water.
2. Pour the chilled water into your stopped-up kitchen sink.
3. Now set the flask on a stove burner. When the water is boiling, hold the flask with the potholder glove and carry it over to the sink. Place the stopper in the flask and tap it once. (Don't push the stopper in!)
4. Now, holding the flask by the stopper, put it all the way into the chilled water so it sits on the bottom of the sink. Keep your fingers on the stopper to hold the flask down. What happens to the water? It keeps on boiling!
5. *After five minutes,* take the stopper out and pour the boiling water out into your hand. It's only warm water!

Why?

The water will boil as long as the stopper remains in place. Why? Boiling occurs when the temperature of a liquid is high enough for bubbles to be able to push out against the weight of the air pushing down. The higher the temperature of the liquid, the more forcefully the bubbles can push out.

When your flask was covered and cooled by the chilled water, the air pressure in the flask dropped lower and lower. As a result, the air pushed less and less on the water below, making it easy for the bubbles in the water to push out (or boil). In other words, the lower the air pressure, the lower the boiling temperature, even if the water is ice cold.

Air Apparent I

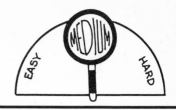

If you can't see the air, how do you know it's there? We take the air's existence for granted, but the ancient Greeks didn't. They wanted to *prove* its existence. Through an experiment very similar to the one you're about to perform (without the plastic soft-drink bottle!), the Greeks did just that. They proved not only that air existed, but that it also exerted pressure.

What You'll Need

- a two-liter, plastic soft-drink bottle with metal cap
- hammer
- nail
- water

Directions

1. With the hammer and nail, punch one hole in the metal cap and one in the side of the bottle, about five inches from the bottom.
2. Now fill the bottle halfway and screw on the cap. Holding the bottle with both hands, turn it upside down. What happens? The water pours out in a steady stream (A).
3. Next, with the bottle still held upside down, cover the hole in the side of the container with your thumb (B). (Be sure not to squeeze the bottle.) What happens now?

Why?

When you turned the bottle upside down and allowed water to pour out, air came in through the punched hole in the side to replace the lost liquid. The air rushing in pushed out more liquid. When you closed up the hole, no air was allowed into the bottle to replace the water. The stream of water quickly came to a stop because the air inside the bottle didn't push as strongly against the water as the air outside the bottle pushed against the cap to keep the water in.

Air Apparent II

By defying gravity, we'll show another way to prove air exerts pressure.

What You'll Need

- plastic cup (no larger than 16 ounces)
- plastic or Styrofoam dinner plate
- water

Directions

1. Set the cup in your sink and fill it with water until it's overflowing.
2. Place the plate face down on the cup.
3. Now, holding the cup in one hand (without squeezing it) and, lightly pressing the plate to the cup with your other hand, turn the cup and plate over.
4. Take your hand off the plate and watch what happens. Wow—nothing! Now gently squeeze the cup.

Why?

Though it may be hard to believe, the weight of the water in the cup does not push as hard *down* on the plate as the air pressure below the plate pushes it *up*. It's as simple as that.

The Air Also Rises

Have you ever seen a beautiful hot-air balloon sailing gracefully in the sky? What keeps it up? It's all in the name.

What You'll Need

- two brown paper lunch bags
- candle
- matches
- ruler
- tape
- one 18" string, two 12" strings

Directions

1. Tie the longer string around the middle of the ruler (at 6" mark) and tape it in place.
2. Tape the other two pieces of string to the bottom of both bags (at center). Then tie the free end of the strings (with bags attached) to the ruler, one at the 1" mark, one at the 11" mark. Tape the strings in place on the ruler.
3. Tape the free end of the long piece of string to the underside of a doorframe.
4. Now light the candle and hold it under one bag. What happens?

Why?

A bagful of hot air is lighter than the same amount of cool air. Thus, the bag filled with hot air rises.

Wonder List

- On a hot day, would the air be cooler near the floor or near the ceiling?

149

High-Wire Act

PARENTAL SUPERVISION RECOMMENDED
Why do you suppose the brave people who walk the high wire at the circus use a balancing bar? We'll let you perform your own act and see.

What You'll Need

- two identical forks
- cola or vinegar bottle
- needle
- cork (about ¾″ thick at bottom)
- pencil with eraser
- quarter

Directions

1. Place the quarter on top of the bottle opening.
2. Stick the eye of the needle in the center of the bottom of the cork.
3. Now stick the two forks into either side of the cork as shown.
4. Place your high-wire act on the quarter, needle down (A). How long will it stay balanced? Spin it around and bob it up and down like a seesaw. Set the needle on a pencil eraser (no need to push it in) and tilt the pencil in different directions (B). You've got a great balancing act on your hands.

Why?

On a seesaw, the farther you are seated from the center, the harder you push up the other side as you push down. The same principle is at work in your high-wire act. When one fork was tilted down one way, the other fork was lifted up away from the bottle. The lifted fork then pulled down hard to lift the other fork back up. In this way, the needle is kept balanced.

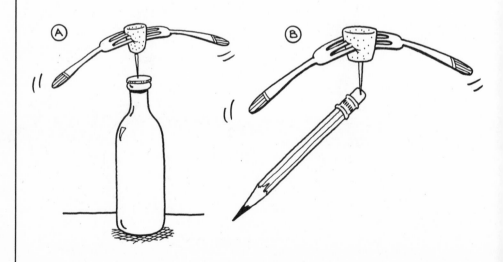

Oil & Water (& Air) Don't Mix

If oil and water (and let's not forget air) don't mix, do you suppose that light travels through them in the same way, or at the same speed?

What You'll Need

- tall, clear glass
- water
- pencil (as tall as the glass)
- cooking oil

Directions

1. Fill the glass three-quarters with water.
2. Pour about one-quarter cup oil into the water. The oil won't want to mix and will bead and float to the surface.
3. Now drop the pencil into the glass. What do you see? The pencil seems to have broken into three pieces.

Why?

Light travels faster in some materials than it does in others. As light travels from one material to another, if it changes speed, it can also change direction (or bend). In your experiment, one edge of the light wave hit the oil boundary first and slowed down. This caused the light wave to change direction. That same light wave then hit the water boundary. It again slowed and changed direction. Since the light is bent, your eye sees the pencil's image as bent.

OIL SETTLES ON TOP

WATER

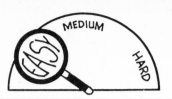
Look around. The world about you (your room, the backyard, the playground) is filled with different colors. Did you know that all these different colors are made of various combinations of just three colors? Can you guess what these "primary" colors are? If you guessed red, yellow, and blue, you'd be right. Let's experiment with color.

What You'll Need

- heavy white drawing or construction paper
- measuring spoons
- medium-sized paintbrush (or use your fingers!)
- red, yellow, and blue tempera paints

Directions

1. Begin by pouring out globs of red, yellow, and blue paint (about a teaspoon each) on the construction paper.
2. Now mix your palette of colors. Start by mixing red with yellow. What color do you get? Wash your paintbrush out, then mix the red with the blue, and then the blue with the yellow. What colors do you get? (Save the colors you created for the Color Wheels experiment.)
3. Next, mix the red, yellow, and blue together. Looks pretty yucky, doesn't it? Experiment by adding various amounts of the three primary colors and you should get . . . black! Would you have guessed that red plus yellow plus blue equals black?

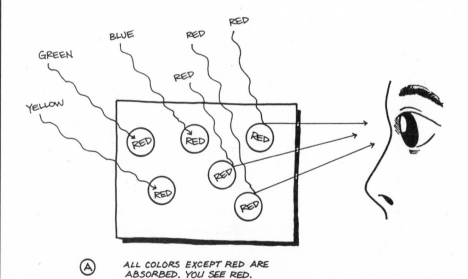

Ⓐ ALL COLORS EXCEPT RED ARE ABSORBED. YOU SEE RED.

When you mix only two primary colors together, you get a "secondary" color. (The orange, green, and purple you mixed are secondary colors.) When you mix *three* primary colors together, why do you get black? The answer has to do with the way materials—all materials—reflect or absorb the colors of the light spectrum. For example, when you see a green leaf, it is absorbing all the spectral colors *except* green (A). In other words, the leaf is reflecting the color green.

Paint is no different than leaves when it comes to color. A glob of red paint absorbs all colors of the spectrum except red. Yellow paint absorbs all colors except yellow, and blue absorbs all but blue. When you mix these colors together, the net result is that *no color* is reflected—in other words, black (B).

Now that you know how to mix colors, your artist's canvas awaits you, Michelangelo!

• In what way is a black hole like a glob of black paint? Because of its incredibly strong gravitational pull, black holes "absorb" light and don't let any reflect back out.

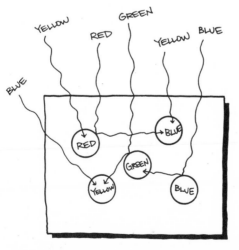

(B) ALL COLORS ARE ABSORBED. YOU SEE BLACK.

Glass-Bottom Boat

Why do tropical cruise boats have glass bottoms? Why do scuba divers wear masks? Let's take a look.

What You'll Need

- large, clean plastic garbage can
- water
- clear glass pie dish or bowl
- various household items

Directions

1. Fill the garbage can with water.
2. Now you get to make your garbage can "party mix." Toss an apple, an orange, a comb, a tin box, a colorful coffee mug—anything that will sink but won't get waterlogged—into the can.
3. Look at your mix at the bottom of the garbage can. How well can you see all that stuff? If you're really daring, poke your head *into* the water and look again. It should be even harder to see the things at the bottom.
4. Now place the pie dish or bowl on top of the water and look again. Can you see any better?

Why?

The surface of a pool of water has bumps and movements that are difficult to see through. (When you put your face in the water, your vision was even worse because your eyes are designed to see not through water but through air.) Placing the glass bowl on the water flattens the water into a smooth surface. Light rays from a flat surface let your eyes focus much more easily.

Phantom Candles

PARENTAL SUPERVISION RECOMMENDED
Create a mysterious illusion in the next experiment, and discover how light interacts with a surface to make phantom images.

What You'll Need

- transparent plastic or acrylic plate (1 sq. ft. x ¼ ")
- matches
- two matching candle-holders, with two candles of equal size (not longer than 8″)
- two narrow books of equal width

Directions

1. Start by placing the two books flat on a table, binder to binder, in a darkened room. Stand the plastic plate between the books.
2. Place one candle (in holder) on each book, about four inches away from the plastic. If there are handles in the holders, line them up so they're facing the same direction.
3. Now light the candles. Standing behind one candle, look through the plastic plate to the other candle. Make sure the candles are lined up.
4. Remove candle 2 from behind the plate, leaving its candleholder behind. A phantom candle appears in the empty candleholder!

Why?

You can see an object only by the light reflected by it. If no light can pass through it from behind, the object will appear solid. If light can pass through it *and* reflect off it, the object will appear ghostlike. In your experiment, the plastic allowed light reflected off of candleholder 2 to pass through it. It also reflected some of candle 1's light back to you, creating a ghostlike image of the candle in candleholder 2. Note: The reflection in the plastic will appear as far *behind* the plastic as the true object is in *front* of it.

Wonder List

- If you want to create a more dramatic phantom image, place two identical chairs on opposite sides of a glass door, at equal distances from it. Then, holding a candle in the dark, seat yourself in one of the chairs.

CANDLEHOLDER #1   CANDLEHOLDER #2

Why Isn't the Sky Green?

We take for granted that the sky is blue, but why is it so? Why does it change color from dawn to noon to dusk? And why isn't it purple or green, or even colorless? As every good scientist knows, there are reasons for everything.

What You'll Need

- glass fishbowl (or a deep glass bowl)
- water
- flashlight
- two thick books
- measuring spoon
- milk

Directions

1. Fill the bowl with water and set it on a table in a darkened room.
2. Stir in two tablespoons of milk and you have recreated the sky.
3. Place the flashlight on the books about three feet away from the bowl. Shine the light directly into the "sky."
4. Crouch down and look into the bowl at eye level with the light behind you (but not blocked). What color does the "sky" appear?
5. Move slowly around the bowl until you're at the opposite side. Look through the bowl to the flashlight. What color is the "sky" now? It's amazing what a little more distance from the light will do!
6. Try holding the flashlight in your hand near the bowl now. What colors do you see as you move the light around and above the bowl?

Why?

Remember that light behaves like waves in many ways. We can understand why the sky is blue by looking at how ocean waves are affected by obstacles. Think about a wave of water moving on the surface of the water. If the wave hits a rock on the water, two different things can happen: If the rock is much smaller than the wave, the wave doesn't even notice and continues in the same direction almost completely unaffected. But if the rock is the same size or even larger than the wave, the wave bounces off and is thrown in a different direction. This effect is called "scattering."

Scattering is what happens to light in the earth's atmosphere. The air molecules are like the rocks, and the different colors of light are the different-sized waves. (Unlike ocean waves, however, unless light gets scattered, you can't see it.) Red light is made of big waves. Since the air molecules are small compared to these, the red light travels through the air without being scattered about. The same holds true for yellow and green light. Blue light, however, is made up of much smaller waves. When they hit the air molecules, they are bounced off in all directions. The result is that everywhere you look, you see blue.

At sunrise and sunset, when the sun is close to the horizon, the light reaching us travels through a greater thickness of atmosphere than when the sun is high overhead, where the air is thinner. When the atmosphere is thick, it contains more dust, air molecules, and water vapor with which to scatter light. The blue light (and green, too!) is scattered so much that we can't see it anymore. But now we are able to see the orange and red light, whose large waves can be scattered by the thick air.

Wonder List

- On Mars, the particles in the air are much bigger than in our atmosphere. So, the longer red waves crash into the air molecules and get scattered about. That's why the Martian sky appears red.

Getting Nowhere

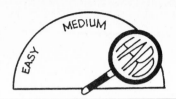

PARENTAL SUPERVISION RECOMMENDED
Picture a spinning bicycle wheel. You can usually tell the direction in which it's spinning, but if the wheel is going fast enough, a strange thing happens. The wheel may actually appear to stop or, even more strangely, to spin backward.

What You'll Need

- heavy white cardboard or matte board (10" x 10" or larger)
- one long nail (about 2" long and thin enough to fit inside spool)
- three small nails

- black felt pen
- piece of board (1 sq. ft. or larger), at least ½" thick
- scissors
- spool of thread (2" high)

- ruler
- protractor
- screw
- pencil
- any kind of tape
- string (18" long)

Directions

1. Using the scissors, pencil, and protractor, cut a circle (5" diameter) out of the cardboard. Mark the center of the circle.
2. With the ruler, draw four lines through the center of the "wheel" to create eight sections of equal size. Fill in four of the pie-shaped pieces with the black felt pen. Add a black dot to one empty pie piece (A).
3. Tape the thread on the spool in place so it won't unravel. Then poke the long nail all the way through the center of the top side of the wheel. Now drop the nail through the center of the spool (B).
4. Holding the paper and spool in place, nail the three small nails into the spool to secure it in place (C). Turn the wheel so the spool faces up, and the long nail will fall out.
5. Poke the nail through the circle about one-half inch from the outside of the wheel. Feed the string through this hole (C).

Ⓐ

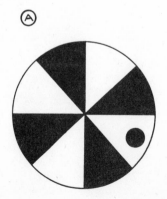

Ⓑ

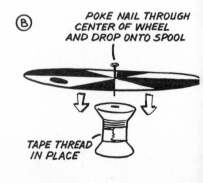

POKE NAIL THROUGH
CENTER OF WHEEL
AND DROP ONTO SPOOL

TAPE THREAD
IN PLACE

6. Tie a "grip knot" on the wheel side of the string. On the spool side of the string, tie another knot, this one around a screw. (The screw acts as a weight.) Tape the screw in place on the underside of the wheel (C).
7. Drive the long nail through the board, and set the spool on top of it (C).
8. Hold the grip knot and gently turn the wheel around in circles. As you turn it faster and faster, what happens to the pie pieces on the wheel? Experiment with spinning the wheel at different speeds. At certain speeds, why do the pie pieces appear to go backward?

Why?

Your brain can perceive (or see) motion only so fast. If an object is moving faster than that, you will only see parts of it. Your brain can observe twenty-four changes in motion per second. Movies are a good example of this. For every second you watch a movie, twenty-four frames whiz by. If there were fewer or more than twenty-four frames, the action would seem unnatural.

As you sped up your spool-wheel, at one point it simply spun too fast for your brain to see. Before then, your brain could observe the full motion of the wheel. But why would the wheel appear to go backward? For one thing, the wheel would have to be going fast enough (say, several cycles per second) so you couldn't follow the black dot as it traveled around it. Then, let's say that the last split-second your brain saw the wheel was when the black dot was pointing toward noon. If the next time you saw the wheel the dot was not clockwise of noon, but, say, at 11 o'clock, the wheel would appear to be going backward. If the next time your brain sees the dot it's at 10 o'clock, then 9 o'clock, and so forth, the wheel will seem to be going backward.

Wonder List

- A strobe light has the reverse effect of the spinning spool-wheel. Instead of giving your brain too much information to perceive, the strobe light, in blacking out portions of information, gives your brain too little to perceive.

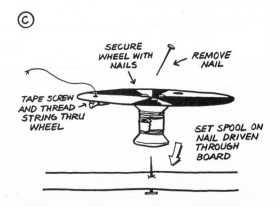

Ⓒ

SECURE WHEEL WITH NAILS

REMOVE NAIL

TAPE SCREW AND THREAD STRING THRU WHEEL

SET SPOOL ON NAIL DRIVEN THROUGH BOARD

Color Wheels

PARENTAL SUPERVISION RECOMMENDED

Now let's examine how your brain *sees* colors. We don't mean in just an ordinary way, but when you set your colors spinning.

What You'll Need

- paints (primary and secondary colors)
- paintbrush
- protractor (or dinner plate for tracing)
- transparent tape
- scissors
- pencil
- white construction paper
- the spool-wheel and board you made in the Getting Nowhere experiment

Directions

1. Using a pencil, scissors, and a protractor, cut out several circles of white construction paper.
2. Draw lines down the center of your "wheels," separating them into halves.
3. On one circle, paint one half red and the other half green.
4. When the wheel is dry, attach it onto the spool-wheel with the tape. Make sure to put tape on either side of the string, which should come out the side between the two wheels (A).
5. Grab the string and spin the wheel faster and faster. What happens to the green and red?
6. Repeat steps 3 through 5, this time painting a wheel blue and orange, then one yellow and purple. What happens to the colors?

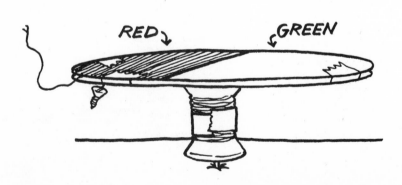

RED   GREEN

Why?

As you learned in Getting Nowhere, when you look at something, your brain keeps a picture of it inside your head for a little while. This is called "persistence of vision." You can see this by grabbing one end of a pencil between two fingers and quickly wiggling it in front of you. If you shake the pencil fast enough, it will appear as if there are two pencils (B). Of course, you know there's only one—the "second" pencil is merely the persistent image inside your head of the real pencil. Your brain hasn't had time to get rid of the first picture before it sees the pencil moved to another position. This is why fast-moving objects appear to blur.

When you turned your color wheel fast enough, your brain didn't have time to get rid of one color before it saw the next color. So, your brain simply combined the two color pictures, just like it combined the two pencil pictures. The interesting thing is that your brain sees rapid, alternating pictures of red and green as white, blue and orange as white, and yellow and purple as gray!

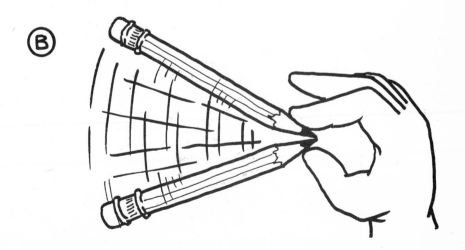

Centuries ago, Sir Isaac Newton made an incredible discovery: light wasn't white at all, but actually many colors of light that combined to look white. This was a major discovery in the field of optics (the study of light). We know a great deal about our universe through the study of the light spectrum.

What You'll Need

- prism
- sheet of white paper
- lamp (without shade)

Directions

1. Experiment with the prism in normal light by holding it up to your eye and viewing several objects. You'll see that the light reaching your eye from these objects *disperses,* or separates, into colors.
2. Now hold up a piece of paper near the lamp light, and look at its edges through the prism. How many different colors can you see?

Why?

In outer space (in a vacuum), all the different colors in a beam of light travel at the same speed. As a result, they stay combined and are seen as white light. But when light travels through glass, the different colors travel at *different* speeds. One color outruns another, and they begin to separate. As they spread out, they can be seen individually. It's just like running a race. If everyone runs at the same speed, they will stay together. If everyone runs at different speeds, pretty soon the runners are all spread out, just like the different colors of light in a prism.

Wonder List

- Almost everything we know about in outer space—how big stars are, what they're made of—comes from studying the various colors of light given off by stars. This area of study is called "spectrum analysis."
- You can see the spectrum—a rainbow—by spraying a fine mist from your garden hose into the air with the sun behind you.

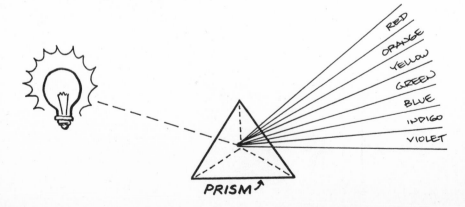

PRISM

It's the Wave!

We know that white light can split into its various colors, but can it disappear into blackness? (And we don't mean by turning off the light switch!) Read on.

What You'll Need

• nylon stockings (black or another dark color works best)

Directions

1. Take one stocking leg and hold it up to the light as shown. Notice the patterns and waves of light and dark?
2. Stretch the nylon in different directions and see the patterns change.

Why?

Many things in nature behave like the waves in the ocean. When two waves smash into each other, they form a bigger wave. If a bump in a wave collides with a dip in the wave, the wave disappears. This "disappearing wave" is easy to understand if you compare it to a hole in the ground. The dirt dug out of the hole forms a mound (bump) next to the hole (dip). The mound is like the crest of the wave, and the hole is like the trough. When a mound meets a hole, the mound fills the hole, and what are you left with?

Light also travels in waves. Just as a bump and dip in the water can make each other disappear, so can two light waves. You can't see the light waves, but you can see how a material affects them. When the light traveled through the nylon mesh, it combined in all these ways: bump to bump, dip to dip, and bump to dip. These interactions are called interference. When a light bump fell into a light dip, the light disappeared—darkness. These are the dark areas you saw. The light areas are where two bumps or two dips combined.

Wonder List

• Two sound waves can cancel each other out and produce . . . silence.
• Interference patterns are used to create three-dimensional holographic images.

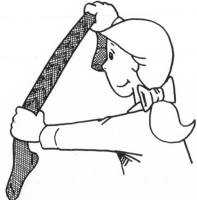

163

Optical Illusions

Optical illusions help reveal how your brain works. Sometimes your brain will interpret an unfamiliar image as being familiar, even though it's *mis*interpreting it. That's why optical illusions are fun—you get to catch your brain making a mistake! Look at these illusions and see if you can figure out why your brain mistakes what it sees.

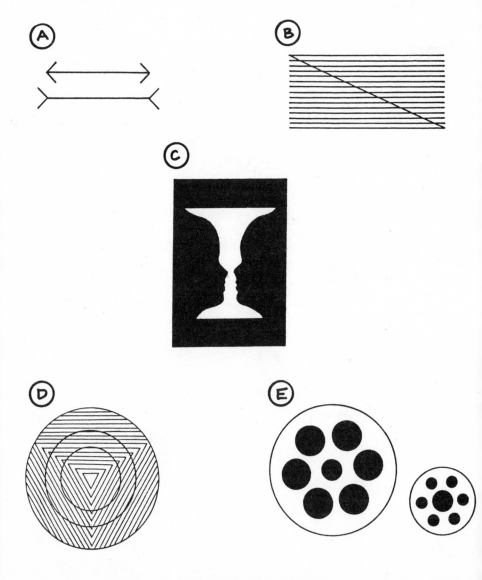

A. Both lines are the same length.   B. the diagonal line is straight and unbroken.   C. You see either a vase or two faces.   D. The concentric circles are perfect circles.   E. The two center circles are the same size.

What's the Sense of It?

You know the world around you only through your senses. But did you know that your senses can sometimes fool you, giving you a misleading picture of the world? In this experiment, we'll explore the sensation of touch.

What You'll Need

- three large bowls
- ice cubes
- a clock or watch with second hand
- water

Directions

1. Fill the bowls with water: the first bowl with very hot water (not boiling), the second with lukewarm water, the third with ice water.
2. Dunk your left hand into the hot water and your right hand into the ice water at the same time. Have a partner clock fifteen seconds while you keep your hands fully immersed.
3. Now place both hands into the lukewarm water at the same time. What happens? How would you describe the sensation your left hand feels? What about your right hand?

Why?

Sometimes your senses measure something very different than you think they do. For example, you may think that what feels hot has a high temperature or that what feels cold has a low temperature. But your body doesn't measure temperature. (If it did, when you placed your hands in the lukewarm water they would have felt the temperature as the same, but they didn't.) What you feel, instead, is the *change* in temperature and how fast that change is occurring—that is, how fast you receive or give away heat energy.

Receiving heat feels hot, and the faster you receive it, the hotter it feels. Giving heat away feels cool, and the faster you give it away, the cooler it feels. Since heat always travels from the hotter object to the cooler object, your cold right hand received heat from the lukewarm water, so it felt warm. Your warm left hand gave away heat to the lukewarm water, so it felt cool.

Sweet-and-Sour Science

Do you know where your sweet, salty, sour, and bitter taste centers are? Let's explore the sense of taste and answer this question.

What You'll Need

- sugar
- instant coffee grains
- vinegar
- measuring spoons
- cap from vinegar bottle
- table salt
- plate

Directions

1. Pour your ingredients into separate piles on a plate. You'll need a quarter teaspoon each of salt, sugar, and coffee, and a capful of vinegar.
2. Wet your finger, dip it into the salt and place your finger in the center of your tongue—not too far forward and not too far back. Keep your finger in place and your mouth open (closing your mouth will spread the taste to other parts of your tongue). Can you taste anything?
3. Now move your finger to a salty taste center. What happens now?
4. Repeat steps 2 and 3 with the sugar, coffee, and vinegar. (For best results, rinse your mouth out before moving on to a new taste.) When experimenting with sugar, move your finger to the tip of your tongue; with the coffee, to the back of your tongue; and with the vinegar, to either side and slightly back. Did you taste anything by touching the center of your tongue? What about when you moved your finger and struck a taste center?

Why?

Did you know that all tastes—from banana to barbecue chicken to cheddar cheese—are a combination of any or all of the four "primary" tastes (remember the Reflections on Color experiment)? You can test this by creating a combo-taste. Dip one finger into the sugar and the other into the vinegar. Now place both fingers in your mouth at the same time and close your mouth. Can you taste the sugar and vinegar mixing? Does it remind you of a Chinese dish you had recently? Presto—sweet-and-sour finger!

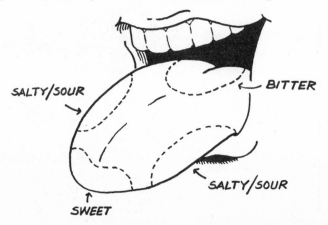

Tickle Your Feet

Why can't you tickle yourself? If someone else tickles you, why do you become unbearably ticklish? The answers are not as easy as you think!

What You'll Need

- a ticklish partner

Directions

1. Working with a partner, try to tickle yourselves in your most ticklish spots. Not much fun, is it?
2. Now it's time to tickle each other for a minute or two. If you were paying attention, your partner identified his or her tickle "hot spot," so . . . one, two, three, go!
3. After the two of you have recovered, try to explain why you couldn't tickle yourself but your partner could. Any ideas?

Why?

One reason for not being able to tickle yourself is physical. When you tickle yourself, your brain has two streams of touch sensations to deal with: those coming from the area you're tickling, and those coming from the hand doing the tickling. When *someone else* tickles you, your brain has only one stream of sensations to process. Your brain can concentrate on the tickling sensations alone. But believe it or not, tickling has more to do with psychology than with your sensation of touch. When someone else is about to tickle you, there are a few silly seconds of anticipation before the tickling begins. This anticipation makes your brain focus attention on the tickling sensations you're about to experience. You "tune in" more, so you actually have a heightened experience of the sensations.

167

Invisible Ink

PARENTAL SUPERVISION REQUIRED

Treasure maps and scientific formulas, escape plans and code secrets—you can't let just anybody see these things. No, for these kinds of schemes, you just have to have invisible ink!

What You'll Need

- bottled lemon juice
- paintbrush
- very long stick matches
- notebook paper

Directions

1. Make up a secret message for your best friend. Then, with the paintbrush and lemon juice, paint your message on the paper.
2. Set the paper aside to dry (sunshine will speed up this process).
3. When the message is dry, your friend can decode it. (It's a good idea to decode the message over a sink.) While one person holds the paper, the other person should light the match and sweep it in small circles about an inch under the paper. Be careful not to hold the match in one place for more than a second. After a few moments, the secret message will appear.

Why?

The lemon juice contains a chemical that burns much more quickly than paper. So, before the paper has a chance to heat and ignite, the lemon juice burns, revealing the secret message.

I C 3 D

Your brain is constantly trying to make sense of the information it receives. In the next experiment, you will be able to *see* your brain trying to sort out confusing visual images.

What You'll Need

- 8½″ x 11″ white construction paper
- ruler
- colored pens
- various household items with a circular edge, varying in size
- scissors
- 8½″ x 11″ sheet of paper
- a partner

Directions

1. First, create a "vision separator" for yourself. Hold the construction paper against your face and have a friend outline your profile (A).
2. Cut along the line, and you'll have a piece of paper that fits over your forehead, nose, and mouth that separates your vision.
3. Now draw a vertical line down the center of the sheet of paper.
4. Using two different-colored pens, draw two circles (the size of cola cans) on opposite sides of the line (B).
5. Place your vision separator along the vertical line of the paper, fit your profile into the separator, and look at the circles. What happens to them?
6. This is one you can play around with. Experiment by drawing the different shapes shown in C, or make up your own.

Why?

To determine an object's position correctly, your brain requires both of your eyes (stereoscopic vision). The vision separator took away your brain's ability to determine position. Because the images *looked* the same, and their position was unclear to your brain, your brain thought they were a single image. That's why it tried to fuse them.

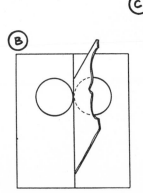

Password

Your mind favors the familiar. That is, your brain sees what it is used to seeing. It loves patterns. For example, as you learned to read, your mind became familiar with common sentence structures and sounds. But your mind can trick you, and in the following experiments, we'll show you how. After you've played these word games, try them on a friend or family member.

Directions

1. Read the following sign out loud.

> A frivolous feline of Fenwith,
> Donned her finest of furs to fetch men with.
> First the frog of St. Fly
> On the Fourth of July,
> Then the fish of Fifeshire on the Fifth.

2. Now count the number of f's in the limerick (before you read further). How many were there? Did you count sixteen? Seventeen? Would you believe there are actually twenty f's in the rhyme? Which ones did you miss?

3. Next read the following sign out loud.

king
of the
the jungle

4. Write what you read on a piece of paper. Now compare what you wrote against the sign. Are they the same? Look very carefully and you'll see that there are two "the's" in the phrase. Chances are you missed the second one both when you read it aloud and compared your written version against it.

Why?

If you're like most people, when you counted the f's in the first sign you missed the f's in each word "of." Because the word is pronounced as though it were spelled "ov," your mind literally did not see the "f" even though it was right in front of your nose.

In the second sign, you didn't see the second "the" because you're not used to seeing two "the's" in a row in English. In fact, your brain recognizes a different pattern: only one "the." So your mind skips right over the second "the"!

Know Your Way

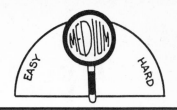

PARENTAL SUPERVISION RECOMMENDED

Next time you go backpacking or hiking, bring a needle, a magnet, and matches. If you ever become lost and no one has a compass, you'll be a hero!

What You'll Need

- cork (about ½" wide)
- horseshoe magnet (6-lb pull)
- knife
- match
- needle
- pencil

Directions

1. Cut off the bottom end of your cork (like you're slicing a carrot). Then cut a notch down the center of the flat side of your cork chip.
2. Press the needle lengthwise into the notch.
3. Light a match and heat one end of the needle until it is hot. Then touch it to your magnet (A).
4. Dip the needle into the water to cool it, then drop your cork chip into the center of the bowl of water, with the needle side down. What happens? You've made a compass!
5. Using a pencil point, rotate the needle away from its position, then let go. Your compass will spin back to north. Hold a magnet around and above the compass and watch what happens (B).

Why?

Heating the needle makes it easier for the little north and south poles inside the needle to line up with the magnet's poles. When it cools, the poles stay lined up, leaving the needle magnetized.

Ⓐ HEAT NEEDLE, THEN TOUCH TO MAGNET Ⓑ

Static Charge

Almost everything you experience results from a quality of microscopic particles called "charge." Charged particles are responsible for the strange attractions and repulsions between objects. Moving charges create magnetic forces, while static charges create electric forces.

What You'll Need

- a plastic rod (acrylic or plexiglass, 1 ft. long x ½ " wide)
- a silk scarf
- sheet of notebook paper
- rubber glove

Directions

1. Tear up the sheet of paper into tiny bits. Spread the bits on a table so they're not touching each other.
2. Put a rubber glove on one hand and hold the plastic rod with it. With the other hand, rub the silk scarf vigorously up and down along the rod for a few seconds.
3. Hold the rod close to the paper bits. What happens? Move the rod in circles over the paper bits and watch them dance and fly!
4. Experiment by moving the paper bits nearer and farther apart on the table. Don't forget to rub the rod now and then with the silk.

Why?

When it comes to charged particles, it's true that opposites attract. A negative charge attracts a positive charge, and vice versa. When it comes to *same* charges, though, the attraction is over. Two negative charges repel (push away) each other, as do two positive charges.

The plastic rod and silk were chosen for this experiment because of their natural qualities. When you rub the plastic with the silk, the plastic strips off negatively charged particles (electrons) from the silk. Thus, by rubbing the rod you are "charging" it. The rubber glove prevents the charged particles from coming off the rod onto your hand.

When you approach the paper bits, the negative charges on the rod attract the positive charges in the paper. The paper leaps up to the rod (so fast, though, that you have to watch carefully to see it). Once the paper and rod touch, however, the negative charges on the rod rapidly leak onto the paper. (Can you guess why? Because the negative charges on the rod are trying to get away from each other!) Some of the paper immediately becomes negatively charged. Given that same charges push each other away, what would you expect to happen next? The paper and rod repel each other. The rod is too heavy to go anywhere, but the paper bits are light enough to shoot away.

Wonder List

- Try holding up the charged rod to your hair. It's also fun to go into a dark room and hold the tip of the charged rod to your finger.

Creating a Force Field

What do magnets and electricity have in common? Plenty! They're different aspects of the same physical structure. Create a magnetic field and see.

What You'll Need

- two D-size batteries
- the compass you made in Know Your Way
- insulated wire, 20″ long (22-gauge "bus" wire or larger, stripped ½″ on either end)
- tape
- bowl of water

Directions

1. Tape the two batteries together, positive end to negative end.
2. Coil the center of the wire around your finger and twist it once. Leave about three inches of wire free at either end, and tape these ends to the metal ends of the batteries.
3. Fill a bowl with water and drop in the needle compass you made.
4. Dip the loop of wire into the water and watch what happens to your compass. This time you've made a magnetic force field!

Why?

In your experiment, the battery pushed charged particles (electrons) through the coil of wire. These moving electrical charges created a magnetic field, which could affect the compass you made. In a simple magnet, this is exactly what happens. The charged particles move within the iron and create a force field that attracts metal objects.

The Human Antenna

What You'll Need

- television set
- screwdriver
- a human body (you'll do nicely)

Directions

1. Turn your television on and tune in to a station with clear reception.
2. Your television set has two antenna connections labeled "VHF" (which stands for very high frequency) on the back. Using the screwdriver, loosen these connections and detach the antenna wires. What happens to the picture on the screen? Your TV reception should be distorted and snowy.
3. Have a friend or parent watch the screen as you perform the next step. Extend your left arm out to the side, and, using the index finger of your right hand, touch one of the two connections.
4. Now switch places with your partner and repeat Step 3. What happens to the picture when your partner touches the screw?

Why?

An antenna is a device that collects electromagnetic signals and then sends them to an "electronic box" to be decoded—in this case, your television set. The larger the antenna, the more signals it can collect. The screw on the back of your television set is too small to collect many of the signals, so the reception is poor. Your body, however, can collect many more signals. By touching the screw, your body can then send them to the television's electronics, resulting in a much better picture.

Wonder List

- In astronomy, why are bigger telescopes better?
- Did you know that your eye behaves like a miniature antenna? It collects electromagnetic information (in the form of light), and the pupil, by getting larger or smaller, controls the amount of information coming in.

Stop the Music

All around you at every moment there is information in the air waiting to be decoded. Music and pictures from faraway lands, tales of distant galaxies, the life and death of stars—all this and more exist in the form of electromagnetic waves, the kind of waves picked up by a radio, television, or telescope. Most of the time, this wave energy goes unnoticed. But with the right kind of "magic box," you can explore new worlds. In the next two experiments, we will explore some of the properties of these waves, and we'll answer two questions concerning this invisible realm: Is it ever possible to escape these mysterious waves? Can the waves really travel through you?

What You'll Need

- a transistor radio (battery operated)
- aluminum foil

Directions

1. Turn your radio on and tune it to a station that has a clear signal.
2. Now tear a piece of aluminum foil long enough to completely wrap the radio, including the antenna.
3. Sit the radio on top of the foil, then slowly raise the sides of the foil until they meet and overlap above the radio. What happened to the reception? Why did the radio stop playing?

Why?

A radio is a "magic box" that selects particular waves out of the shower of electromagnetic waves around us. One way to shield out radio waves is to surround the radio with a conductor (a metal, such as the aluminum foil). The charged particles in the conductor move around in response to the waves to neutralize them. When the waves are neutralized, your radio suddenly has no more information to decode.

By the way, have you ever noticed that plug-in radios don't have antennas? That's because the cord acts as an antenna. Signals from space can reach your radio through the electrical wiring in your home into the radio cord. To "stop the music," you'd have to shield your entire home!

Wonder List

- If people from another planet were trying to communicate with us, what kind of "magic box" would we have to build to hear them?*

- Signals reaching us from distant galaxies and stars allow us to see back in time—wow!

*This question is too fascinating to leave unanswered. As a matter of fact, scientists have developed a superhuge radio telescope for just the purpose of "hearing" signals from other planets. The program is called the Search for Extra-Terrestrial Intelligence, or SETI for short.

The Invisible Made Visible

You will see mysterious magnetic forces at work in this experiment.

What You'll Need

- horseshoe magnet (6-lb pull)
- sheet of heavy construction paper or thin cardboard
- iron filings
- a partner

Directions

1. It's best to work over a table on this one. Start by holding the construction paper horizontally with one hand.
2. With your other hand, hold the magnet underneath the paper with the end of the horseshoe facing up.
3. Have a partner slowly pour the iron filings onto the paper in a sweeping fashion. Notice the very particular pattern the filings fall into.
4. Slide the magnet all around the underside of the paper. Carefully observe how the magnet affects the filings. How would you describe their behavior as you move the magnet?

Why?

Iron is a magnetic material, which means that it can be affected (pushed or pulled) by another magnet. A big piece of iron would be too heavy to be pushed or pulled by a small magnet, but the tiny iron filings in your experiment were light enough to move easily in response to the magnetic forces of the magnet. When you poured the filings onto a piece of paper held close to the magnet, you made a map of a portion of its "magnetic field"—that is, the region of space affected by the magnet. This magnetic field is usually invisible, but by pouring the filings you made the invisible visible!

Wonder List

- Would sawdust react to a magnet the way iron filings do? Why are some materials magnetic and others not? What mysterious things go on inside a magnet?

- In a compass, where is the magnet making the compass needle point north? Can you guess what it is? It's the earth! The earth happens to be a gigantic magnet.

141

Hot Socks

Have you ever wondered why people wear light-colored clothes in the summertime? Did you ever stand barefoot on a hot asphalt playground and then run like mad to find relief on the white lines? In the following experiment, you will observe and understand why black heats up in the presence of light.

What You'll Need

- a pair of white socks
- a pair of black socks
- a bright lamp, with removable shade (optional)

Directions

1. You'll need a warm sunny day for this one (but a strong lamp will do if a sunny day refuses to appear). Start by putting your black socks on one hand and foot, and the white socks on the other hand and foot.
2. Find a spot where the sunshine is clear and strong, sit in a comfortable position with your feet stretched out, and read about some of the other experiments in this book. Notice anything happening to the hand and foot with the black socks on? (You can achieve the same effect by holding your sock-covered hands about four or five inches away from a 100-watt light bulb. Be sure not to stare at the light!)

Why?

In the Reflections on Colors experiment, we showed that "black" really means that a substance is absorbing all colors of light and reflecting none. The light being absorbed has energy (it comes from the sun). When it is collected, this energy can heat things up. Thus, the black sock (the asphalt, black clothing, etc.) absorbs and collects the light energy and heats up your foot. On the other hand, the white sock (the white painted lines, white clothing, etc.) reflects most of the light (and its energy) away from you.

Wonder List

- We usually think of outer space as extremely cold, so why do the astronauts wear white space suits?

The Light Barrier

We know that electric current flows through metal, but will it flow through water? You can rig up a flashlight to answer that question.

What You'll Need

- flashlight
- two 10″ pieces of insulated wire (22-gauge)
- clear glass bowl
- distilled water
- salt
- measuring spoons
- a partner
- tape
- two copper plates

Directions

1. Unscrew and remove the flashlight lid and take the contents out. Tape the two batteries together (positive end to negative end).
2. Have an adult strip ½″ of the insulation off both ends of both wires.
3. Tape one wire end to the negative end of your two batteries. Tape another wire end (from the second piece of wire) to the circle of metal (usually copper) in the light bulb piece.
4. With a long piece of tape, attach the flashlight bulb to the positive battery end as shown. Test that your flashlight works by touching the two free wire ends together. (It's okay to touch these exposed ends; not enough current is traveling through them to do any harm.)
5. Have a friend hold the copper plates in the bowl. Now touch the free wire ends to the plates. Does your flashlight flash on?
6. Add salt slowly and watch what happens.

Why?

A material allows electric current to flow (or conduct) when there are charged particles (electrons) inside it that are free to move. In a normal light bulb, for example, the electrons in the bulb's tiny wire (called the filament) can flow easily. This flow heats the filament until it glows white hot and the bulb shines. However, when the electrons inside a material are held tightly in place, no current can flow. This is what happens with distilled water, which is an insulator (it cannot conduct electrons). Adding salt stripped some electrons away from the water, allowing them to move around the copper plates, then through the wires to the filament to light the bulb.

TOUCH WIRES TO PLATES

HOLD COPPER PLATES IN WATER

Don't Take Sides

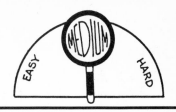

PARENTAL SUPERVISION RECOMMENDED

We usually think of objects as having at least two sides. For example, a piece of paper has a front and a back, and a loop has an inside and an outside. Do you think it is possible for something to have only one side? We're going to make the famous Möbius strip (named for its inventor) and see.

What You'll Need

- sheet of construction paper
- scissors
- pen, pencil, or colored marker
- ruler
- transparent tape

Directions

1. Cut a strip of paper that is 1″ wide and 10½″ long.
2. With the ruler and pen or pencil, mark off sections on the strip of paper. Your first mark should be ¼″ from the left end of the strip. Draw a vertical line through it. From there, tick off 1″ increments until you reach the other end of the strip, where you'll have ¼″ remaining. There, draw another vertical line (A).
3. Now number your inches 1 through 10 as shown. Take the bottom of the strip and flip it up and over to the other side of the strip.
4. Repeat steps 2 and 3, this time numbering the inches from 11 to 20.
5. Now, holding the ends of the strip, twist it once, then join the ends. Overlap the ends exactly ¼″ and tape the ends in place on both "sides" (B).
6. Voilà! You've just created a loop with only one side. How did you do it? If you don't believe you've got a one-sided loop, count the numbers on your strip starting with 1. When you reach 11, the opposite side of your strip, you'll find no flipping is required to keep counting to 20.

Wonder List

- Can you think of anything else with just one side?*

*Neither can we.

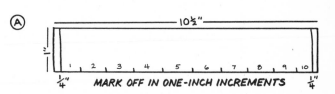

Ⓐ

MARK OFF IN ONE-INCH INCREMENTS

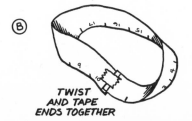

Ⓑ

TWIST
AND TAPE
ENDS TOGETHER

Musical Bottles

Have you ever wondered why the tuba, with its booming voice, is such a large instrument, and why the piccolo, with its tiny voice, is such a small instrument? What does sound have to do with size? Let's see. . . .

What You'll Need

- six empty glass bottles (same size)
- water

Directions

1. Fill the bottles with varying amounts of water, from nearly empty to nearly full. Then line the bottles up as shown (A).
2. Blow across the top of each bottle, one by one, starting with the bottle with the least water. What happens to the sound pitch as you move from bottle to bottle?
3. Now repeat your music-making, this time moving fast as you blow across your row of bottles in one breath.

Why?

Sound is actually vibrations, or waves, in the air. The faster the waves vibrate, the higher the sound pitch. The slower they vibrate, the deeper the sound pitch. How long or short the waves are has to do with how fast or slow they vibrate. The rapidly vibrating, high-pitched waves are short, while the slowly vibrating, low-pitched waves are long. If the waves have a large space to vibrate in, they will be longer than if they have a small space to vibrate in.

A good way to see this is by taking hold of one end of a garden hose (leaving the other end attached to the faucet) and shaking it up and down. When you shake the full length of the hose, the vibrations in it are slow and long. (If the vibrations were sound, the hose would have a deep voice!) When you shake a shorter length of hose (say, shorter by ten feet), you'll see that the vibrations are faster and shorter. (Here the hose would have a higher voice.)

This is exactly what happened in your musical bottles. The larger the space in which the air could vibrate, the longer and slower were the vibrations (B). So, the deepest sound came from the bottle with the least amount of water and the most air. The smaller the space in which the air could vibrate, the shorter and higher were the vibrations (B). So, the highest sound came from the bottle with the most water and the least air.

Wonder List

• Compare the sounds made by a bottle being filled with those of a bottle being emptied. The "glug-glug" sounds of the first will start low and end high. And of the second?

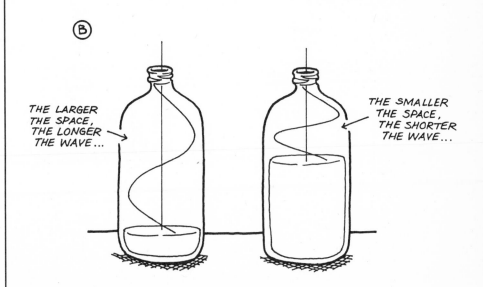

Ⓑ

THE LARGER
THE SPACE,
THE LONGER
THE WAVE...

THE SMALLER
THE SPACE,
THE SHORTER
THE WAVE...

145 Learning Topsoil Conservation

Before they knew that topsoil was the most valuable soil for agriculture, farmers used to let topsoil wash away. Much fertile land was destroyed. You can see for yourself how this might have happened by comparing an old farming method with a new one designed to conserve topsoil.

What You'll Need

- two half-gallon milk cartons
- two books (or pieces of wood) each about an inch thick
- scissors
- two sprinkling cans (or pitchers)
- two buckets
- dirt or potting soil
- ruler
- a partner
- water

Directions

1. Cut off one side and the top of the two milk cartons. Then cut the remaining sides and bottoms so they're four inches high.
2. Fill your cartons with dirt and shape it into mounds that taper down at the open end of the carton. Set the cartons at the edge of a table, the back ends on books, and place the two buckets below to catch dirt and mud.
3. In carton 1, furrow three parallel lines down the length of the dirt mound. In carton 2, furrow one winding, continuous line.
4. Now your miniature "farms" are ready for a rainstorm. With a partner assisting you, simultaneously trickle about a pint of water from the sprinkling cans into both cartons. Which "farm" holds the most water?

Why?

Carton 2 demonstrates the modern "contour" farming method. Since the furrow is longer, it is better on two counts: the water has more time to be absorbed by the dirt, and less topsoil is washed away. If you lift both cartons, carton 2 will feel heavier because the dirt was able to absorb more water.

Super Sleuth

Here's an experiment that will let you play detective and teach you something about a very important tool in crime investigation—fingerprinting.

What You'll Need

- one teaspoon fine carbon powder (if necessary, a piece of charcoal ground up with a mortar and pestle or hammer will do)
- mixing bowl and spoon
- a fine-haired cosmetic brush
- transparent tape
- white paper
- ceramic plate or blow
- one teaspoon baking soda
- magnifying glass

Directions

1. In a mixing bowl, combine the baking soda and carbon and mix thoroughly.
2. Now you or your partner gets to play international jewel thief and leave your fingerprints behind. A ceramic plate or bowl works well for this. (By the way, newly washed hands will not leave the best of prints behind.)
3. With your magnifying glass, inspect for fingerprints. Find anything?
4. Now dip the cosmetic brush into the carbon mixture and *very lightly* dust the ceramic surface. Inspect the area with your magnifying glass. Now what do you see?
5. Place a piece of tape over the fingerprint to "lift" it. Rub the tape gently, then place the tape on a piece of white paper. You should have a close-to-perfect fingerprint for your crime files. Make fingerprints of several people and line them up to compare.

Why?

The natural oils in your hands stick to surfaces, leaving fingerprints behind. The oils aren't very visible, but the carbon mixture clinging to the oils is. Since no two fingerprints are alike, when a set of prints is found during a criminal investigation, there can be no doubt who the culprit is!

Show Me the Light

PARENTAL SUPERVISION RECOMMENDED

What will a plant do when deprived of most of its sunlight? Like all living things, it has to adapt to its new environment. In the following experiment, you will see for yourself what we mean.

What You'll Need

- a syngonium "arrow leaf" plant from your local nursery
- scissors or knife
- cardboard box, tall enough to cover the plant without bending the leaves
- sheet of notebook paper
- pen or pencil

Directions

1. First cut a 3″ square "window" in one side of the box.
2. Now find a sunny spot indoors where you can leave your plant undisturbed for several days. Carefully observe the position of your plant's leaves. In which direction are they facing? They should be facing all different directions. Note the information on the paper, which you can call your "Helio Log" (*helio* in Greek means "sun").
3. Now place the box over the plant. Note on the log the date and time you covered the plant as well as the direction the window is facing. Keep your plant covered at all times, except for the few moments when the syngonium may need watering. No peeking!
4. Here you get a break from this experiment. Go try the next experiment—it's fun!
5. After approximately 48 hours, uncover your plant. Notice anything different about the leaves? How and why have the leaves shifted direction? Record your observations in your Helio Log.

Why?

You can think of sunlight as the food of plants. Without sunlight, plants will neither grow nor live long. Through a process called photosynthesis, plants convert sunlight energy into a form they can use as food. In this sense, sunlight is not unlike the oxygen that we need to survive (see the Fuel for

Thought experiment). When imprisoned in the darkness of a box, your plant was literally starved of nutrition. So, naturally, it had to adapt to its new environment. To drink up the only sunlight available, the plant turned its broad leaves toward the window. How long do you think your plant could survive with only this windowful of light?

Wonder List

- Why is it that the foliage of most trees is not at the base or even the middle of the tree, but at their very tip-tops?

Fuel for Thought

PARENTAL SUPERVISION RECOMMENDED
When you see a lighted candle, the wick is the fuel for the flame. Is that all the candle needs to burn?

What You'll Need

- candle
- matches
- a clear glass, tall enough to fit over candle

Directions

1. Light the candle.
2. Place the glass over the candle. Can you guess what will happen to the flame?

Why?

A burning candle is a chemical reaction. Like many other reactions, it needs oxygen to continue. In this experiment, the flame went out because it needed oxygen to continue burning the fuel (the wick).

Wonder List

- A burning candle is much like human metabolism. Metabolism is the process by which food and other substances are converted into energy that the body can use. Oxygen is a very important part of that process, and without it, metabolism couldn't occur.

Mystical Crystals

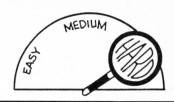
PARENTAL SUPERVISION REQUIRED

Have you ever seen a glistening geode with its lavender, green, or blue crystals sparkling in the light? Crystals are among the most beautiful of all structures. Their very precise shape comes from the precise way in which their atoms stack up like building blocks. Other substances such as glass have no such regularity, so they lack the special crystalline appearance.

What You'll Need

- 500-ml Erlenmeyer flask (with rubber stopper)
- sodium acetate, powdered, with no impurities (nontoxic)
- ice cubes
- funnel
- measuring spoons
- flashlight
- stove burner
- water
- 8″ test tube (with 8-cup volume)
- plastic straw
- tall glass
- glove potholder

Directions

1. Fill the flask half full with water and set it on a stove burner at medium heat. You'll want the water to be boiling by the time you get to step 4.
2. Make a "solution" (a mixture) of water and sodium acetate (which is a kind of salt). Pour two tablespoons of lukewarm water into the test tube.
3. Now, using the funnel and measuring spoon, bit by bit pour three-and-a-half teaspoons of the sodium acetate into the test tube. After pouring each teaspoon, cover the tube with the stopper and shake. You'll find that by the time you get to the last half teaspoon, your solution is "saturated," and not all of the salt will dissolve.
4. Next, drop the test tube into the Erlenmeyer flask with boiling water in it (A). After a couple of minutes, pour another four-and-a-half teaspoons of the sodium acetate into the solution. Stir the mixture with the straw after each teaspoon to dissolve the salt.
5. Place two ice cubes in a tall glass of water. Then, with the potholder, lift the test tube out of the flask and place it in the glass (B).
6. After 90 seconds, drop a small pinch of the salt into the test tube and watch what happens (C). Don't take your eyes off the tube. Hold the flashlight up to the crystals. Wow!

Ⓐ

7. To repeat the experiment, just return the test tube to the flask, watch the crystals melt, then repeat steps 5 and 6.

Why?

Just as a building needs a first block to build on, a crystal needs its first block to build on. The building blocks for crystals are usually tiny particles. When you first poured the sodium acetate into the water, the water molecules grabbed on to the salt atoms, and the salt disappeared. But at a low temperature, the water can grab on to only so much salt. To get it to grab on to even more salt, you needed to increase the water temperature. So, as the water became hotter, it could pull even more salt atoms into the solution.
You then cooled the solution in the glass of cold water. All the salt that wouldn't dissolve at the lower temperature suddenly became available to make crystals. Here is where the building blocks came in: Before the salt atoms could make crystals, they needed something to grab on to (build on). Pinching in a bit of the salt provided the first block on which the salt crystal could grow. Once that happened, another crystal could build onto the first, and then another onto the second, and then in a matter of seconds, presto! Crystals . . .

Wonder List

• All of computer electronics is based on the controlled growth of crystals. Have you heard of silicon? It's a crystal!

Ⓑ

Ⓒ

ADD PINCH OF
SODIUM ACETATE
AND WATCH!

SODIUM
ACETATE

Cloud in a Jar

PARENTAL SUPERVISION RECOMMENDED

Clouds are amazing things. One minute the sky is clear, and the next minute an immense cloud is looming toward you. They can be wispy or billowy, dangerous or harmless. But how do clouds form? Let's make one and see.

What You'll Need

- piece of rubber ⅓ " to ¼ " thick, cut in a circle to fit within the rubber ring inside pickle jar lid
- matches
- needle valve (for blowing up basketballs, etc.) and pump
- stick incense
- a glass pickle jar
- a partner
- hammer and nail

Directions

1. Nail two holes in the jar lid, one toward the outside of the lid (the "finger hole"), one in the center (the "valve hole") (A). Punch these holes from the inside out.
2. Push the nail through the center of the rubber to make a narrow hole.
3. Now put the needle valve first through the valve hole in the lid, then all the way through the rubber hole (B).
4. Attach the pump to the needle valve.
5. Put about one-half inch of water in the jar and swish it around.
6. With the jar held tilted at an angle, light the incense and stick it inside the jar for about three seconds (C). Then quickly pull it out and place the lid on the smoke-filled jar.

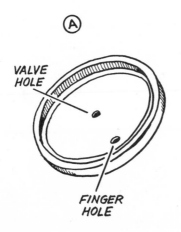

Ⓐ

VALVE HOLE

FINGER HOLE

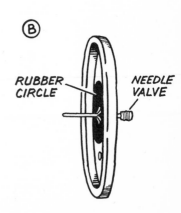

Ⓑ

RUBBER CIRCLE

NEEDLE VALVE

7. Have your partner hold the jar and cover the finger hole tightly. Then, pump air into it five times. The smoke will clear as you pump.

8. As you watch the jar very carefully, have your partner uncover the finger hole. Poof!

Why?

Why?

Clouds form when the air pressure and temperature in the atmosphere drop suddenly. This allows condensation, or the formation of water droplets from vapor, to occur. (You can see condensation form on a glass of cold water left standing in a warm room.) But just like crystals in the previous experiment, the water vapor in the air needs something to grab on to (usually dust or soot) before it can become a water droplet. The smoke particles in your experiment supplied the building blocks for the droplets. The water vapor in the jar wanted to condense into droplets, but it couldn't because the air pressure was too high. Releasing some of the air out of the jar (by uncovering the finger hole) caused a sudden drop in pressure and temperature and . . . pop! A cloud was born.

Wonder List

- In drought-stricken areas, farmers will sometimes purposely "seed" a cloud by dropping solid particles into it. The water vapor in the cloud will condense onto the particles and form water droplets—rain!

- Would you guess that among the most disastrous aftereffects of a volcanic eruption are mudflows? Why?

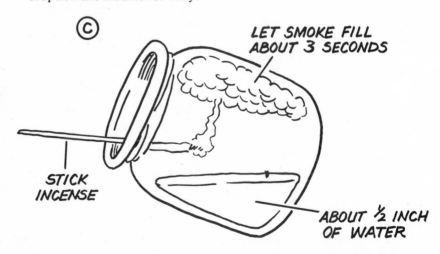

© LET SMOKE FILL ABOUT 3 SECONDS

STICK INCENSE

ABOUT ½ INCH OF WATER